THE CONSTITUTIONAL REFORM SERIES

General Editor
Robert Blackburn
Reader in Public Law, King's College, University of
London

PUBLIC SERVICE REFORMS

ISSUES OF ACCOUNTABILITY AND PUBLIC LAW

DAWN OLIVER

AND

GAVIN DREWRY

PINTER

First published 1996 by
Pinter, *A Cassell Imprint*
Wellington House, 125 Strand, London WC2R 0BB, England
127 West 24th Street, New York, NY 10011, USA

British Library Cataloguing in Publication Data
Oliver, Dawn
    Public service reforms : issues of accountability and
    public law. – (The constitutional reform series)
    1. Public utilities – Law and legislation – Great Britain
    I.Title II.Drewry, Gavin
    344.1'039

    ISBN 1 85567 391 6

    Library of Congress Cataloging-in-Publication Data
Oliver, Dawn
    Public service reforms : issues of accountability and public law /
Dawn Oliver and Gavin Drewry.
        p.   cm. – (Constitutional reform series)
    Includes bibliographical references and index.
    ISBN 0–18–557391–6
    1. Administrative law–Great Britain.   2. Public administration–
Great Britain   3. Great Britain–Politics and government–1979–
I. Drewry, Gavin. II. Title. III. Series.
KD4879.044.   1996
342.41'06–dc20
[344.1026]   96–529
                                                                        CIP

Printed and bound in Great Britain by Biddles Limited, Guildford and King's Lynn

Contents

Preface

This book is the product of a long-standing friendship and collaboration between two academics from different disciplines, with a shared interest in the nature and the implications of public sector reform. It has been a feature of British public administration that civil servants, nurtured in a 'generalist' tradition, are not expected to know much about administrative law. Perhaps partly for this reason, it has been a feature of scholarship in this subject-area that a wide academic divide separates the interests and contributions of public lawyers and those of political scientists. Both disciplines have generated a lot of research and a lot of writing that is relevant to the subject, but (with a few honourable exceptions) British political scientists seldom seem to read public lawyers' writings, and vice versa. Cross-disciplinary collaboration is a rarity. This book seeks, in a modest way, to bridge that gap.

The subject of reform of the public sector – the most recent phase of which, sometimes referred to as the New Public Management Revolution, has been characterized by an emphasis on private markets rather than public bureaucracies as the best basis for service delivery – has an international dimension. The decentralization and contractualization of public services have important legal and constitutional implications, particularly in relation to the issue of accountability. Yet in Britain, where there is no codified constitution, where the Civil Service has no statutory basis and where central government is run largely on the basis of the royal prerogative and ministerial fiat, these implications have been largely ignored.

Only after nearly two decades of reform, and perhaps stimulated by Britain's increasing involvement with the European Union and with countries that have written constitutions and more legalistic cultures, is the realization beginning to dawn that the traditional forms of accountability, based on ministerial responsibility to Parliament, may need to be reassessed, and the New Public Management to be matched by a new administrative law. This is the main theme of this book, and we hope that it will be of interest to students both of public law and of politics and public administration.

The authors would like to thank Mike Fogden, the Chief Executive of the Employment Service, Ron Oliver, Chief Executive of the Vehicle Inspectorate, Peter MacDonald, Director General Corporate Services of Her Majesty's Stationery Office, and Chris Southgate, Director Publications of Her Majesty's Stationery Office, for interviews and information about their agencies in 1995, as well as colleagues and friends whose comments have contributed to the end result. The responsibility for the product, however, is entirely ours.

Dawn Oliver
Gavin Drewry
September 1995

NOTE: The manuscript for this book was completed in September 1995. Since then there have been a number of important developments, some of which we have tried to incorporate into the text without having to revise too radically.

1

The Changing Landscape of Public Administration: Issues of Accountability

The years since 1979, when Margaret Thatcher became prime minister, have been particularly associated with radical programmes to reform public services – both substantively, in terms of the nature and range of services provided by the state, and institutionally, in terms of the way in which service provision is organized and funded. This book is concerned primarily with this period and in particular with the first half of the 1990s, after Thatcher departed from office.

However, before proceeding further, two caveats must be entered. The first is that use of the word 'programme' begs important questions about the coherence of these reforming exercises; one must be careful to avoid the temptation to see, with hindsight, the unfolding of a grand design that may simply not have existed at the time in the hearts and minds of ministers. There have of course been published programmes of reform, set out in election manifestos and elsewhere, and one can identify some underlying themes that link them together, but these themes are not always as coherent or as clearly defined as some apologists for the Thatcher–Major years, or indeed as some anti-Thatcherite conspiracy theorists, might like to pretend.

The second caveat is that the pursuit of public service reform was not of course *invented* in 1979. The famous 'Three Es' (efficiency, effectiveness and economy), which were such a prominent slogan of the Thatcher years, have always featured, in some form or other, on the modern political agenda. The efficiency scrutinies conducted in the early 1980s by Lord Rayner's Efficiency Unit, designed to eliminate wasteful practices in Whitehall, are in some ways redolent of Gladstone's preoccupation with the 'saving of candle ends', more than a century ago. All modern governments have, to a greater or lesser extent, and for a variety of reasons, had their own programmes for reforming public

1

services. Every incoming administration likes to be distinctive and to distance itself to some extent from the actions and priorities of its predecessors, and – either as a direct object of policy (e.g. abolishing the Greater London Council or launching the 'Next Steps' programme or setting up an Office of Public Service) or as a by-product of other policies (e.g. setting up a new agency to administer a statutory child support scheme) – leaves its own special mark upon the machinery of government.

Our purposes in this book are to sketch the theoretical and political background to these reforms and consider the implications for accountability of some of these public service reforms, focusing particularly on the development of new mechanisms of accountability (often variations on old ones) which can complement or substitute for the established conventions of individual ministerial responsibility to Parliament, and collective ministerial accountability to the public through the ballot box.

Two linked sets of arrangements which have been central to the reforms, the executive agency or 'Next Steps' initiative in the Civil Service and the Citizen's Charter, provide case studies from which lessons can be drawn about the working of public service reform. Comparative material from two other countries, New Zealand and Sweden, highlights some of the special features in the changed British public administration landscape. This material provides a basis for considering whether and how arrangements for securing appropriate accountability could be improved so as to promote high standards of service, accountability, responsiveness to the needs of the public, and efficiency and effectiveness in this country.

In the rest of this introductory chapter the concepts of *accountability* and *responsibility* as they operate in relations between ministers, civil servants and Parliament will be explored. In Chapter 2 we set the institutional and technical reforms to public services in the context of the themes and theories that have influenced them. In the following chapter we give brief overviews of some of the techniques adopted by government with a view to achieving 'economy, efficiency and effectiveness' – the Three Es – in public services, including some discussion of the Citizen's Charter. An account will then be given of some of the important institutional changes that have been introduced in the period since 1980, in which the executive agencies provide our main focus. In Chapter 4 we provide an overview of some of the principles and problems associated with public sector reform, introducing themes that are considered in subsequent chapters and anticipating points that emerge later from the comparative study and from the findings of our case studies. We shall then, in Chapter 5, seek to summarize the legal basis for public administration and the statutory and other law-based accountability mechanisms available, identifying the points at which the law stops and political accountability is expected to take over. In Chapter 6 we consider the role of Parliament in the control of a changing public service. These discussions will lay the foundations for three case studies in the operation of the executive agencies in Chapter 7, and a comparative study of arrangements in Sweden and New Zealand in Chapter 8. In the concluding chapter we pull the threads of our argument and findings together and consider the possibilities for improving accountability arrangements.

ACCOUNTABILITY AND RESPONSIBILITY IN GOVERNMENT

Use (and sometimes misuse) of the term 'accountability' in the context of discussions about politics and government is far from new, but it has become something of a 'buzz word' in the last decade or so (Marshall, 1984; Day and Klein, 1987; White et al., 1994). It is an ambiguous word, often misleadingly used interchangeably with 'responsibility'. The concepts of responsibility and accountability are linked, but they are not interchangeable. The ambiguity is particularly problematic in relation to public service reform.

One difficulty in considering accountability is to determine the criteria against which a person is to be held accountable. If we take accountability to mean the duty to give explanations or justifications for action and then to make amends if it should turn out that something has gone wrong, the mechanism will be weak if the criteria are not articulated, as is often the case in relation to political or administrative accountability. When ministers are said to be 'accountable' to Parliament, does this mean that they are expected to justify action in terms of its legality, its procedural fairness, its efficiency, its wisdom or its ideological soundness – or some combination of these criteria?

It is in recognition of such weaknesses and ambiguities in accountability that a trend has developed in the last few decades to 'codify' the standards of conduct expected of ministers or civil servants – and indeed local government councillors and others – and the performance outputs expected. Examples of codification include *Departmental Evidence and Response to Select Committees* (Cabinet Office, 1994), known as the Osmotherly Rules after the civil servant who wrote the 1980 version. The use of framework documents for executive agencies and the 'citizen's charters' are further manifestations of this trend, which is in effect a form of 'normativization' of politics and administration with a view to establishing standards and enhancing accountability. Such codification is, as we will see later, something of a novelty in British public administration, much of which has traditionally been based on un-written conventions and understandings, and on the exercise by ministers of the surviving elements of the royal prerogative, inherited from the long-gone days of absolute monarchy, rather than on legislation and formal codes.

Other issues arise over the identity of the body to which a person is responsible. The British system relies heavily on the doctrine that civil servants are responsible to ministers, and ministers are responsible to Parliament and through Parliament to the people. We shall explore the different meanings of responsibility and accountability and the implications of the doctrine later in this chapter, but it is important to note at this point that other mechanisms of accountability are built into the British system apart from the doctrines associated with ministerial responsibility – there are bodies other than Parliament, and some of them quite separate from Parliament, to which ministers, civil servants and other public officials and bodies are accountable. These other bodies apply a range of criteria in imposing accountability, and they have a variety of procedures and different sanctions from those that are imposed through conventions relating to ministerial responsibility. As we shall see in our comparisons with New Zealand and Sweden in Chapter 8, it is possible for governments in advanced Western parliamentary democracies to operate responsibly and accountably without the degree of reliance on ministerial responsibility to Parliament that exists in Britain.

By way of brief summary of these alternatives to civil servants' responsibility to ministers and ministerial responsibility to Parliament and ultimately the electorate, bodies funded substantially out of public funds are accountable to the Comptroller and Auditor General and, via the National Audit Office, to Parliament; the criteria applied in this kind of accountability relate to the legality and propriety of expenditure and to value for money, and sanctions include findings that expenditure has been improper, which may then result in adjustments to the financing of the department and parliamentary criticism of the responsible minister or the responsible accounting officer (the latter being a civil servant) and even surcharge. Local authorities are accountable to the District Auditor and Audit Commission for their stewardship of public money, and findings of improper expenditure can result in surcharging of councillors and their disqualification from office – sanctions which do not have an exact parallel in central government. Government departments are also subject to internal audit procedures applied by the Treasury, again concerned with the propriety of expenditure and the maintenance of sound financial management.

Bodies performing public functions are accountable to the courts through the judicial review jurisdiction for the legality of their actions, and the criteria applied by the courts are, briefly summarized, those of technical legality, procedural propriety, rationality and fairness. Sanctions include the quashing of decisions, or orders that legal duties be performed (Chapter 5). Public bodies are also accountable to the courts if they breach the ordinary law of the land, as they may be sued for breach of contract and for tort, subject to certain exceptions to take account of their special constitutional position.

Where an individual complains of maladministration in the way he or she has been treated by a government body, the possibility of complaint to a statutory 'ombudsman', the Parliamentary Commissioner for Administration (the PCA), arises, via a Member of Parliament (MP): the criteria applied here are elaborations of the concept of 'maladministration' and do not include illegality. The PCA investigates and makes findings of fact and recommendations to the department in question, which are not strictly enforceable though they are generally complied with (see Chapter 5). National Health Service (NHS) patients and individuals aggrieved by local government action also have access to ombudsmen. And there are generally internal complaints procedures in most public bodies dealing with members of the public.

Hence we can see that accountability and responsibility are by no means confined to political mechanisms, and it will be an important part of our argument that attention needs to be paid to developing non-political mechanisms to meet the inevitable weaknesses of ministerial responsibility in our constitutional arrangements – weaknesses that have been highlighted and sometimes exacerbated by recent public sector reforms.

MINISTERS, CIVIL SERVANTS AND PARLIAMENT

There are subtle differences between accountability and responsibility which have to some extent been fudged by the establishment of Next Steps agencies headed by chief executives (for a description of the Next Steps programme, see Chapter 3). According to the Osmotherly Rules, para. 42:

> Where a Select Committee is investigating matters which are
> delegated to an Agency in its Framework Document, evidence
> will normally be given by the Chief Executive. Like other
> officials, Agency Chief Executives *give evidence on behalf of the
> Minister to whom they are accountable and are subject to that
> Minister's instruction.* (Emphasis added.)

The House of Commons Treasury and Civil Service Committee (TCSC) has objected to this approach and expressed the view that chief executives should be directly responsible to the House of Commons select committees and not even theoretically responsible only through the minister (TCSC, 1987–8, HC 494, para. 46). The First Division Association (FDA) – which represents senior civil servants – has agreed with the TCSC on this (*ibid.*: para. 47).

In its report of 1994 on *The Role of the Civil Service* the TCSC again urged its view about the accountability of chief executives:

> We do not believe that Ministerial power to intervene in the actions and decision of Agencies justifies the retention of Ministerial accountability for the actions and decisions of Agencies for which the Chief Executives are responsible ... The delegation of responsibility should be accompanied by a commensurate delegation of accountability. *We recommend that Agency Chief Executives should be directly and personally accountable to Select Committees in relation to their annual performance agreements. Ministers should remain accountable for the framework documents and for their part in negotiating the annual performance agreement, as well as for all instructions given to Agency Chief Executives by them subsequent to the annual performance agreement.* (para. 171; emphasis added)

On this approach, ministerial responsibility should remain to the extent that if things were to go badly wrong Parliament would expect the ministers to put things right, possibly by dismissing the chief executive or revising the framework document. But, subject to that, civil servants themselves should be responsible. Though subsequently rejected by the government in its White Paper, *Taking Forward Continuity and Change* (Cm 2748, 1995: 31), this view is gaining ground in the light of experiences of lacunae in responsibility with the Prison Service and the Child Support Agency, which are discussed later.

THE SEPARATION OF ACCOUNTABILITY FROM RESPONSIBILITY

The principles on which the lines between accountability and responsibility are drawn are not clear – particularly in the British context. In a book published more than thirty years ago, A.H. Birch noted that usage of the term 'responsibility' to signify the accountability of individual ministers or of the government as a whole to an elected assembly 'is more common in Britain than in most other countries' (Birch, 1964: 20).

As long ago as 1954, in the aftermath of the famous Crichel Down case, the then Home Secretary, Sir David Maxwell Fyfe, distinguished between different kinds of ministerial responsibility that can arise from the actions of civil servants. He opined, for instance, that:

where action is taken by a civil servant of which the Minister disapproves and has no prior knowledge, and the conduct of the official is reprehensible, then there is no obligation on the part of the Minister to defend what he believes to be wrong ... But, of course he remains constitutionally responsible to Parliament for the fact that something has gone wrong, and he alone can tell Parliament what has occurred and render an account of his stewardship. (HC Deb., 20 July 1954: vol. 530, col. 1286)

This was an important refinement of the antique and fanciful fiction – long overtaken by the development of a modern interventionist state and the vast bureaucracy that grew up with it – that a minister should take the blame for everything that happens in his or her department, whether or not he or she knows about or approves of it. But it still leaves important demarcation issues unresolved – and has been overtaken by recent developments, in particular the development of Next Steps agencies in which chief executives are both responsible and, increasingly, answerable for 'operational' matters.

Since 1994 ministers have been seeking to refine the distinction between 'responsibility' and 'accountability', as the extract from the TCSC report given above shows. By 'responsibility' the government means the job or set of functions that a person – the chief executive of an agency, for instance – has to do and the idea that he or she may be expected to take the blame in some way if mistakes are made; the implication of this is that ministers are not 'responsible' for the actions of others. By 'accountability' ministers mean (implicitly echoing the Maxwell Fyfe formulation, above) that they have control over the giving of explanations or justifications of what is being done in their departments, and possibly a duty to see that matters are put right once they have gone wrong, without necessarily accepting any blame or culpability which might call for an apology or resignation by the minister. The control over explanations and justifications is exercised by their claim to have the exclusive right and duty to explain or justify, or to direct civil servants as to how they may answer questions from select committees about such matters. As the extract from the Osmotherly Rules quoted above shows, civil servants are not entitled to answer for themselves as opposed to on behalf of their ministers.

The exclusivity of ministerial accountability was put to the TCSC in its inquiry into the role of the Civil Service in 1994. They rejected it:

We do not believe that Ministerial power to intervene in the actions and decisions of Agencies justifies the retention of Ministerial accountability for the actions and decisions of Agencies for which Chief Executives are responsible. The theoretical separation of accountability and responsibility is nowhere more untenable than in the operation of Agencies; continued adherence to the theory behind such a separation might jeopardise the durability of the delegation at the heart of Next Steps. The delegation of responsibility should be accompanied by the commensurate delegation of accountability. (TCSC, 1993–4, *The Role of the Civil Service*, HC 27-I: para. 171)

The distinction between accountability and responsibility was considered further by the government in its White Paper *Taking Forward Continuity and Change* (Cm 2748, 1995), its response to the TCSC report. The government stated that:

a Minister is 'accountable' to Parliament for everything which goes on within his Department, in the sense that Parliament can call the Minister to account for it. The Minister is responsible for the policies of the Department, for the framework through which those policies are delivered, for the resources allocated, for such implementation decisions as the Framework Document may require to be referred or agreed with him and for his response to major failures or expressions of Parliamentary or public concern. But a Minister cannot sensibly be held responsible for everything which goes on in his Department in the sense of having personal knowledge and control of every action taken and being personally blameworthy when delegated tasks are carried out incompetently, or when mistakes or errors of judgement are made at operational level. (p. 28)

This approach leaves open the question of who is responsible, and to whom, when incompetence or mistakes or errors occur at the operational level. The issue arose in the Westland affair: a politically sensitive confidential letter from the Solicitor General had been leaked by officials at the Department of Trade and Industry (DTI). There were doubts as to whether or not the leak had been authorized by the Secretary of State, and there were also some suspicions about the possible complicity of the prime minister herself. The House of Commons Defence Committee investigated the matter, but the government refused to allow the relevant officials to give evidence (the Head of the Civil Service appeared instead), or to disclose how the leak had taken place. It seemed that no officials had been disciplined. There was a possibility therefore that an error had been made or misconduct had occurred at an operational level, and that no one had taken responsibility for it. The Defence Committee found this 'extraordinary' (Fourth Report from the Defence Committee, 1985–6, HC 519; Woodhouse, 1994: 207–13; Oliver and Austin, 1987; Drewry and Butcher, 1991: 4–7).

The attempt to maintain the separation between responsibility and accountability surfaced again, in the Next Steps era, in the row over the escape of prisoners from Parkhurst prison on the Isle of Wight in January 1995. The Home Secretary maintained that he was not responsible for the escape because it was not his job to keep the prison secure, and he could therefore not be held to blame for it. Operational matters of this kind were not his business. He told the House of Commons that:

> With regard to operational responsibility, there has always been a division between policy matters and operational matters. That has existed not only since the introduction of agencies – it has been recognised for years, and indeed for generations. (HC Deb., 10 January 1995: col. 40)

Policy on prison security, funding, etc. were his 'responsibility', but as there was no criticism of those matters he could not be held to blame in any respect. He was 'accountable' in that he needed to establish the facts and explain them to Parliament, and he should do what he could to make sure that security was improved and to 'make amends' for the escape. In this case he did not recognize any duty to resign because he was not personally to blame. The General Secretary of the Association of First Division Civil Servants commented that the Home Secretary had 'no constitutional authority for this claim' (*The Times*, 12 January 1995). She relied in support of her view on the document published by the Cabinet Office in 1992, *Questions of Procedure for Ministers*, which provides:

> Each Minister is responsible to Parliament for the conduct of his or her department, and for the actions carried out by the Department in pursuit of Government policies or in the discharge of responsibilities laid upon him or her as a Minister.

We can see here how the ambiguity of the two terms can be exploited. The term 'responsible' in *Questions of Procedure* has been in the text for many years, well before the concept of 'accountability' had become, to the extent it has now, part of the vocabulary of discussion of relations between ministers and Parliament. While there may once have been a 'golden age' when ministers were expected to take the blame for operational failures, the strong trend for at least forty years has been against this (Marshall, 1984; Finer, 1956; Woodhouse, 1994). In effect the Home Secretary was claiming both that he was not to be regarded as to blame, and that no one other than himself could be required by Parliament to explain what had happened: this approach is an essentially defensive one, designed to frustrate Parliament's efforts to impose responsibility and accountability on public servants.

The Prison Service saga continued following the publication in October 1995 of the Report of the Learmont Inquiry into prison security, which concluded that the Parkhurst escapes 'revealed a chapter of errors at every level and a naivety that defies belief' (Learmont, 1995, para. 2.257). In a House of Commons statement on the day the Report was published, the Home Secretary noted that it 'had not found that any decision of mine, directly or indirectly caused the escape' (HC Deb., 16 October 1995: col. 31). He then announced that the Director General of the Service, Derek Lewis, had 'ceased to hold his post with effect from today' (*ibid.*: col. 33).

Critics, including Lewis himself, were quick to point out that Learmont had also found that the Director General had been regularly distracted from his operational responsibilities by constant ministerial demands for information and advice: the Report called for an in-depth study of the relationship between the Home Office and the Prison Service Agency 'with a view to giving the Prison Service the greater operational independence that Agency status was meant to confer' (Learmont, 1995: para. 3.87). Questions were also raised about the transfer of the Governor of Parkhurst the previous January, it being alleged that the Home Secretary had put pressure on the Director General to take this action, notwithstanding that it was an operational matter. An Opposition motion in the Commons, deploring the Home Secretary's unwillingness 'to accept responsibility for serious operational failures', was comfortably defeated (HC Deb., 19 October 1995: cols. 502–50), but this did little to dispel unease, in Parliament and elsewhere, about the artificiality of the policy/operational distinction in an area of such high political sensitivity.

The point about the extent of a minister's accountability and responsibility was also taken up in relation to the Child Support Agency (CSA) in 1994–5. The CSA – an agency of the Department of Social Security (DSS) – had been set up in a hurry with insufficient trained staff; the workload had been heavier than anticipated and consequently there were unacceptable backlogs of work. Very many complaints were made to MPs, who referred a lot of these complaints to the PCA, about the way parents were treated by the agency. A few years earlier similar problems had been encountered when the Disabled Living Allowance had been introduced by the same department, and the point made strongly was that the department, and the minister, should have learned from experience and made proper provision against similar problems arising in the CSA. (As we shall see in the case study on the Employment Service in Chapter 7, managers have been scarred by the experiences of the CSA and concern now arises whenever a new agency or function is established lest the same errors are repeated.)

The issue in relation to the CSA was the extent to which the minister had a duty to take action where there were problems in the operational aspects of the work of an agency due to inadequate planning. The PCA had received so many complaints about the operation of the CSA that he decided that he should not investigate individual complaints unless they raised new aspects of the work of the CSA or had caused the complainant actual financial loss. The Select Committee on the PCA then decided to take evidence on the CSA in the light of the PCA's general criticisms of the planning and preparation for its establishment and its performance. The Select Committee took evidence from the Parliamentary Under-Secretary, the junior minister. (This was the first occasion that a minister had been questioned by the committee on the contents of an ombudsman's report. Normally the permanent secretary would be heard, since he or she is responsible for the efficient admin-istration of the department.) The committee stressed that it had 'never believed ... that Ministers cannot be held to account for the admin-istrative actions of their department' (Third Report from the Select Committee on the Parliamentary Commissioner for Administration, 1994–5, *The Child Support Agency*, HC 199). The minister accepted that he was 'responsible' when things went wrong, but the problem was in deciding how much a minister could rely on civil servants in the department to establish an agency satisfactorily. The report's conclu-sions about the minister's responsibility insisted that it extends into administrative arrangements:

> We consider that Ministers were too easily satisfied with the
> assurances given by officials ... Ministers should have reacted
> more quickly to the situation as problems became apparent.
> They should have sought assurances that, were pressures to arise
> from other sources, lessons had been learned in relation to
> backlog, volume of complaints, dealing with correspondence,
> training of staff. We expect the questioning of agency officials
> by Ministers to be searching and robust and for Ministers to be
> briefed accordingly. We are in no doubt that maladministration
> in the CSA cannot be divorced from the responsibility of
> Ministers for the framework within which it operated. (HC 199,
> 1994–5: para. 27)

On the second reading debate on the new Child Support Bill in March 1995 (the Bill sought to improve the administration of the CSA and the substantive rules they apply), the Parliamentary Under-Secretary of State for Social Security referred to the evidence he had previously given to the Select Committee on the PCA and, accepting the Select Committee's view, stated that:

there are different functions within the Department in terms of the day-to-day responsibility for the running of the agency and the minister's policy-making job. However, I have to take responsibility from the Dispatch Box for everything that the agency might do. But in no sense was I suggesting that it was a hands-off approach, that it was up to the agency and this it was not my problem. (HC Deb., 20 March 1995: col. 105)

It has long been recognized by both practitioners of public administration and academic writers that, whatever the constitutional theory books may say about the demarcation line between the job of an elected minister and that of a non-elected official who is answerable to the minister, in the real world the functions of 'policy making' and 'administration' are tightly intertwined. Clearly it would be unacceptable for a minister to take the line that operational matters are not the responsibility of ministers at all, in the sense that there is no duty to take steps to see that administrative systems are properly established, or to intervene if things are going wrong at the operational level. Many such difficulties may result directly from the way in which an agency is established and resourced, and here a minister should not be able to avoid all responsibility in the sense of blame.

So in the case of the CSA it came to be accepted, with hindsight, that things were bound to go wrong when it was established with inadequate resources and untrained staff, many of them with no relevant previous experience of the kind of work involved, and the minister was regarded as having failed to meet his responsibilities in these matters (see, e.g., HC Deb., 20 March 1995: col. 101, 103).

These concerns about the responsibility of ministers in relation to administration are likely to continue under the Executive Agency initiative (see Chapters 3 and 7), and the signs are that ministers are under pressure from select committees to recognize that a 'hands-off' approach is unacceptable. But select committees have also expressed concern that chief executives are alert to such problems when setting up new operations, and take steps to avoid a repetition of the CSA crisis (see Fourth Report of the Select Committee on the PCA, 1994–5, HC 394: 24; and see Chapter 7, below).

Another set of confusions in the relationship between responsibility and accountability flows from the importance attached to 'accessibility'. The point can be illustrated by the history of the decision taken in October 1992 that the answers of chief executives to parliamentary questions should be published in Hansard (see Evans, 1995). It was novel that people other than parliamentarians should have 'access' to Hansard in the sense that their words and their answers to questions should be published in the record of parliamentary proceedings.

But accessibility in another sense was also at issue: there was pressure from MPs to make sure that the information contained in these chief executives' answers should be accessible in the sense of being readily available to both MPs and persons outside Parliament. Publication in Hansard was pressed for by MPs because it could secure this accessibility, and thus enable MPs to discharge their functions of imposing responsibility and accountability on ministers (Evans, 1995).

CONCLUSIONS

The distinction sought to be made between the two concepts of responsibility and accountability is not easy to sustain, but it is helpful in illuminating the differences between, on the one hand, having a job to do, including making sure that new systems are properly established, and taking the blame when things go wrong (which is responsibility); and on the other hand, having the exclusive right to explain, having a duty to explain, and making amends without accepting blame (which is accountability).

Accountability and responsibility, then, are closely related to one another, though they are not synonymous. Our concern will principally be with the mechanisms for securing that systems work effectively and agencies are properly resourced and staffed; for extracting explanations from ministers or chief executives for what has been done, whether policy or operational; and for obtaining some kind of amends, either for aggrieved individuals or at a higher level of policy or the quality of administration (as in the Prison Service or CSA cases) for the public at large when things go wrong. As we shall emphasize, the formulation of criteria against which performance can be measured, establishing procedures for the 'audit' of performance against criteria and effective machinery for redress of grievances, and accessibility of information are of central importance.

Some of the weaknesses of ministerial accountability have emerged from our discussion of the concepts of accountability and responsibility, and these weaknesses form the basis for our argument that a stronger system of administrative law needs to develop to compensate for the limitations of ministerial responsibility. These limitations have become more apparent as the Next Steps programme and other public sector reforms have unfolded:

- The criteria against which ministers are held accountable for the work of their departments are unarticulated.
- The availability of information to Parliament is limited by the fact that civil servants can only answer on behalf of and subject to direction from their minister, and ministers cannot in practice be compelled to provide information to Parliament.

- Ministers claim the exclusive right to answer for their departments.
- There are ambiguities in the lines of demarcation between the respective responsibilities of ministers and agency chief executives.
- Until a code for the Civil Service is elaborated, and until codes regulate relations between ministers and civil servants, standards of conduct are not clear.
- If a minister chooses not to discipline a civil servant there is nothing Parliament can do about it.
- Parliament has no say in how new services are established – as with the CSA – and hence little power to secure that proper arrangements are made, save by making it clear that it regards the minister's responsibility as extending to securing that proper arrangements are put in place.

In order to explore these issues, we need to consider the themes and theories underlying public sector reform and, in outline, not only the major innovations in the last fifteen years or so in techniques of public management, but also the institutional changes that have marked these innovations, which have begun to introduce novel concepts of accountability and responsibility and new mechanisms for imposing them on government and other public bodies. As we will argue, the process of revising traditional concepts and mechanisms of accountability, in line with the radical transformation that has taken place in public management, may have begun, but it still has a very long way to go.

2

Themes and Theories: Why Reform the Public Service?

The language and the rhetoric of public service reform may change, but many ideas from the past keep resurfacing in new guises: for instance, some of the arguments underlying the Next Steps programme, launched in 1988, are strongly reminiscent of proposals in the Fulton Report on the Civil Service, published twenty years earlier, when Harold Wilson's Labour government was in office.

The Thatcher–Major years have been particularly notable for the extent and the radicalism of public sector reform – covering all parts of the public sector (Stewart and Walsh, 1992). Les Metcalfe (1993: 351–2) notes that:

> incoming governments often express a commitment to
> managerial efficiency. By so doing they hope to avoid having to
> explain where the resources will come from to live up to their
> electoral promises. But, more often than not, enthusiasm for
> reform is short-lived. Political attention shifts to other subjects.
> In Mrs Thatcher's case, this did not happen.

One important reason that it did not happen was that, for Thatcher and her colleagues, public sector reform was integral to their economic strategy. Another was that Thatcher herself was in office for a very long time; Harold Wilson, who accepted many of the recommendations in the Fulton Report, did not stay around for long enough to see them put into effect. Thatcher's successor, John Major, while displaying a less confrontational policy style, continued, and in many respects extended, her programme of public sector reform.

FROM PUBLIC ADMINISTRATION TO PUBLIC MANAGEMENT

A strong influence on public sector reform has been the view (linked to New Right enthusiasms for free market forces: see below) that public sector personnel have a lot to learn from the private sector. One manifestation of this was Thatcher's importation into Whitehall of prominent businessmen – Lord Rayner, seconded from Marks and Spencer in the early 1980s as the prime minister's efficiency adviser, is probably the best-known example – as special advisers, working closely with the prime minister and her senior colleagues.

This increasingly managerial emphasis has meant that old-style public administrators have had to learn new management skills and new vocabularies; public administration has been recast as a 'new public management' (Hood, 1991). According to Rod Rhodes, the central doctrines of the New Public Management are:

> a focus on management, not policy, and on performance
> appraisal and efficiency; the disaggregation of public
> bureaucracies into agencies which deal with each other on a
> user-pay basis; the use of quasi-markets and contracting out to
> foster competition; cost-cutting; and a style of management
> which emphasizes, amongst other things, output targets,
> limited term contracts, monetary incentives and freedom to
> manage. (Rhodes, 1991: 1)

The culture of government and public services has been transformed. As Metcalfe (1993: p. 352) observes:

> Management methods, models and values have been accepted as
> an integral part of the way the business of government is
> conducted . . . in future the questions will be about what forms
> of public management are appropriate rather than whether
> management, as such, is relevant to government.

He also notes that a similar tendency is observable in many other developed countries; a series of public management surveys by the OECD in the 1990s bears out this observation (OECD, 1990, 1993, 1994). In the United States, the book *Reinventing Government* (Osborne and Gaebler, 1992), with its advocacy of competition, empowerment and decentralization, replete with illustrative examples of good practice, mainly at a local level, became a bestseller, and it has attracted some favourable attention in the UK.

There is nothing new in criticizing the lack of managerial competence in the Civil Service – this was, for instance, a central message in the Fulton Report of 1968. But there has been much scepticism about whether off-the-peg business management prescriptions are universally applicable to the public sector. Stewart and Walsh (1992: 3) observe that:

> The image presented of the private sector is seldom based on empirical evidence of how this sector actually works. Rather it is taken from how introductory textbooks in business administration say it should work.

Metcalfe suggests that 'imposing a one-dimensional business management model on all government organisations, regardless of their functions, is liable to provoke cynicism about the intentions behind the reforms rather than engender support' (Metcalfe, 1993: 364). He is particularly concerned about the fact that the management reforms have not kept pace with the increasing complexity of the public sector, and is critical of the inappropriateness of simple business management models to complex inter-organizational scenarios (e.g. the development of quasi-markets in local government and the NHS).

BUREAUCRACY: BOGEYMAN AND SCAPEGOAT

Leaving aside for a moment the ideologies of the New Right and their concern about correcting the allegedly deeply engrained empire-building tendencies of public officials, it may be noted that bureaucracy has always been a convenient and popular target for political attack. When the word 'bureaucracy' entered the vocabulary, in continental Europe early in the nineteenth century, it was commonly the basis for polemical abuse. According to Martin Albrow, in the first academic treatise on the subject, published in 1846, Robert von Mohl, professor of political science at Heidelberg, noted that employment of the word as a term of abuse varies according to the group making the complaint: 'The privileged classes complained of loss of privileges, the commercial classes of interference in commerce, artisans of paperwork, scientists of ignorance, statesmen of delay' (Albrow, 1970: 29). Students of public law in Britain will be familiar with A.V. Dicey's influential *Introduction to the Study of the Law of the Constitution*, first published in 1885, which includes weighty discussion of, among other things, the rule of law and the sovereignty of Parliament. Dicey resists the notion that, even given the rapid growth of government intervention from the second half of the nineteenth century onwards, the English common law, applicable to government and governed alike, should be displaced by the development of a separate system of administrative law, along the lines of the French *droit administratif*.

In 1929 Lord Chief Justice Hewart, a loyal follower of Dicey, launched a fierce attack on 'the New Despotism'. Denouncing the

17

increasing 'pretensions and encroachments of bureaucracy' (Hewart, 1929: v), he asserted:

> that there is in existence, and in certain quarters in the
> ascendant, a genuine belief that Parliamentary institutions and
> the Rule of Law have been tried and found wanting, and that
> the time has come for the departmental despot who shall be at
> once scientific and benevolent, but above all a law unto himself,
> needs no demonstration. (*ibid.*: 14)

Leaving aside Hewart's intemperate language, his concern about the growth of unaccountable bureaucracy, and the decline of parliamentary control, undoubtedly hit a popular chord – in some respects anticipating the New Right thinking that was to come into vogue many years later. What has changed since Hewart wrote is that scepticism about the effectiveness of parliamentary control has increased and alternatives which do not involve increasing bureaucratic control are developing. And doctrinaire objections to the development of a distinctive system of administrative law have long been out of fashion.

With reference to more recent episodes – in particular to an announcement that the Cabinet Office Efficiency Unit had recommended, in November 1993, that top Civil Service jobs should be opened up to an element of open competition – journalist Simon Jenkins notes that:

> A decade of abuse of public administration is reaching a climax.
> Antagonism to bureaucracy is universal. .... Cursing bureaucrats
> has become a national sport. They are pests. The Welsh
> Secretary accuses the Health Secretary of breeding them by the
> thousand. At the Tory conference, the word Brussels required
> only the suffix bureaucrat for the audience to erupt in a
> paroxysm of hate. The BBC is so propped up by bureaucrats
> that its boss, John Birt, must worry that his building will
> collapse without them. The police is 'overbureaucratised', so is
> the Foreign Office, so is the defence ministry, so are the
> universities. (Jenkins, 1993)

Notwithstanding the analysis by Max Weber at the beginning of the century, which sought to depict bureaucracy as a necessary phenomenon of developed societies, founded on a 'rational legal' form of authority, the pejorative usage of the word has proved very resilient. This usage paints an image of self-serving officials, given to obstructing the long-suffering public (whose taxes pay their salaries) with unnecessary red tape, and frustrating the will of elected ministers. It has often been encouraged by those same ministers, seeking both easy and popular targets for abuse and convenient scapegoats and distracters for their own policy failures and mistakes – with the political bonus that civil servants thus stigmatized are not usually allowed to answer back.

These rather negative and pragmatic reasons for public sector reform can certainly be detected in the pattern of recent events, but there are more positive and ideological explanations that are associated in particular with the phenomena of Thatcherism and the New Right.

THE INGREDIENTS OF THATCHERISM

Much has been written about the phenomenon of Thatcherism. It is probably best depicted not as an intellectually coherent and purposively programmatic doctrine, but rather as a series of loosely interlinked propositions and ideas. This is the approach taken by Dennis Kavanagh (1987: 11–12), who isolates eight strands of Thatcher's 'belief system' as revealed through interviews and her conference speeches:

1. the limited capacity of government to do lasting good, but its great capacity to do harm;
2. the importance of individual responsibility and the existence of right and wrong;
3. the state should be strong enough to perform its 'primary' tasks of ensuring adequate defence and law and order;
4. people should solve their own problems rather than turning to the government;
5. increasing public expenditure, without economic growth, involves more taxation and less choice for individuals;
6. the market is the best means of promoting economic growth and promoting free choice and of safeguarding personal liberty;
7. more expenditure on one service usually means less on another, unless one resorts to borrowing or inflation. Each service is paid for by 'hard-pressed' taxpayers, many of whom may be poorer than the beneficiaries of particular programmes;
8. government intervention may be counterproductive in terms of slowing down society's ability to adapt in a changing world.

One manifestation of Thatcherism was the pursuit of tough 'monetarist' macroeconomic policies (inspired in part by the writings of Milton Friedman: see below), giving high priority to the reduction of inflation; while at the same time pursuing market-orientated 'supply-side' policies, designed to stimulate the economic growth by tax cuts, privatization and labour market reforms. Thatcherite economic policy was based on a flat rejection of hitherto orthodox Keynesian ideas that governments can and should stimulate economic growth and reduce unemployment by spending public money on major investment projects. The incoming government was also deeply hostile to the various incomes policies pursued by its predecessors. Part of the impetus for reform of public sector institutions came directly from this commitment to supply-side policies; it also gained indirect impetus from Mrs Thatcher's suspicion that an unreformed Civil Service, reared on old economic doctrines and strongly trade-unionized, would obstruct these new policies.

THATCHERISM AND THE NEW RIGHT

'Thatcherism' is a label that seeks to embrace (and perhaps retrospectively give an appearance of coherence to) an amorphous cluster of political attitudes and policies. The same can be said of the expression the 'New Right', with which Thatcher's brand of Conservatism (and indeed US President Reagan's free market 'Reaganomics' in the 1980s) has often been associated. This has generated a very large academic literature, which is well reviewed by Dennis Kavanagh (1987: Ch. 3; see also Bosanquet, 1983).

Part of the problem in delineating the boundaries of the New Right stems from the fact that the meanings of traditional political terms like 'left' and 'right' and 'Conservative' and 'Liberal' have changed over time and become highly ambiguous – particularly when transplanted from one side of the Atlantic to the other, where they have quite different connotations (Kavanagh, 1987: 103–4). According to some usages, the term 'New Right' itself subsumes variants such as 'neo-liberalism' and 'neo-conservatism'. It is often difficult to fit an individual's ideological position comfortably into one of these slots. Thus many Conservatives who take a strongly neo-liberal, free market, non-interventionist line on economic issues take a much more interventionist and authoritarian neo-conservative line on many social issues – such as education and law and order.

Moreover (as will be described later) Thatcherite–Majorite industrial and economic policies of deregulation and non-intervention have developed alongside highly *interventionist* policies towards many parts of the public sector, such as the Civil Service, local government, the NHS and higher education. The frontiers of the state have to some extent been 'rolled back', but the state itself has become, politically, highly centralized as, in particular, the power of elected local authorities has been whittled away. Stephen Bailey, examining the impact of public choice policies (see below) on local government, points out that current reforms to empower citizens via functional decentralization 'where

20

centrally financed agencies operate within market and pseudo-market systems' contrast with trends towards political decentralization elsewhere in Europe (Bailey, 1993: 8).

Metcalfe argues that there is a sharp contrast beween the New Right rhetoric of market choice and the realities of tight central control:

> The collective outcomes of market processes are supposedly the unintended consequences of individual choices. But whenever these reforms have shown signs of deviating from planned objectives, government has acted to bring them into line. The centre has not just established a level playing field and then stepped back. Instead, it is continually involved in rigging the market. Ironically, a government ideologically committed to relying on market forces has introduced reforms which require increased central control and constant intervention. (Metcalfe, 1993: 366)

Those employed in the public sector (still nearly five million of them in 1996, despite sixteen years of budgetary retrenchment, privatization, contracting out, etc.) find themselves increasingly squeezed between the demands and budgetary disciplines of central government, concerned to achieve better value for money, and the insistence of better-informed consumers, newly 'empowered' by the Citizen's Charter, upon their rights to good service – with recourse to new and/or improved mechanisms for redress of grievances if the product falls short of their expectations. The emergence of new, increasingly market-orientated public services, and new forms of accountability and redress, have important legal and constitutional implications, which will be considered later.

Much New Right thinking derives its inspiration from free market economic theory (some aspects of which can be traced back to the eighteenth-century Scottish economist Adam Smith, whose name was adopted by the influential New Right policy institute, the Adam Smith Institute, established in 1977). Some of that inspiration came from American public choice theory – notably the work of Buchanan and Tullock (1962), Tullock (1965), Niskanen (1971, 1973) and Olson (1965, 1982) – which seeks to provide an economic analysis of politics. Even more immediately influential in a Thatcherite context was the work of two major economists in the classical liberal free market tradition – Friedrich von Hayek (e.g. 1944, 1960, 1973–9) and Milton Friedman (e.g. 1962, 1975) – both of whose writings helped to shape the ideas of many leading Conservatives, including Thatcher herself (Kavanagh, 1987: 10; see also several passing references in Thatcher, 1993). Sir Keith Joseph was a particularly vigorous enthusiast for New Right ideas, and when he became Secretary of State for Industry in 1979

21

he issued a reading list to his officials 'which was dominated by conservative and free market writers, including Hayek, Friedman and von Mises' (Kavanagh, 1987: 96).

Hayek, who won the Nobel Prize for Economics in 1974 and is widely regarded as the founding father of the New Right, strongly opposed economic planning, and throughout his extensive writings on political economy was a consistent advocate of free market principles. He argued strongly against redistributive legislation:

> formal equality before the law is in conflict, and in fact
> incompatible, with any activity of the government deliberately
> aiming at material or substantive equality of different people,
> and ... any policy aimed at a substantive ideal of redistributive
> justice must lead to the destruction of the Rule of Law. (Hayek,
> 1944: 59)

The work of Milton Friedman, another Nobel Prize winner, has a somewhat different and narrower focus than that of Hayek, but had a more direct and explicit influence on both British and American economic policy in the early 1980s. In particular, Friedman played a major part in establishing the Thatcherite counter-Keynesian view that inflation is caused by the supply of money growing faster than the economy as a whole. Monetarist economics was nothing new (the Labour Chancellor Denis Healey had introduced monetary targets, albeit with his arm having been sharply twisted by the International Monetary Fund (IMF), in 1976); but the Thatcher government's elevation of monetarism to a central economic creed – and the rapid rise in unemployment that ensued – was the source of bitter political controversy in the early 1980s.

The main exponents of public choice theory have been Americans. At the core of this cluster of theories is a critique of the view traditionally held by welfare economists that market failure in welfare distribution is sufficient grounds for government intervention. Public choice theorists argue that, on the contrary, state intervention is intrinsically inefficient.

Part of the basis for this position lies in the notion of bureaucratic over-supply. Thus William Niskanen, whose ideas (like those of Friedman) were promulgated by the free market Institute of Economic Affairs in London in the 1970s, argued that bureaucrats, motivated by rational self-interest, will always seek to maximize their own utility by seeking to increase their agency budgets. They are allowed to get away with this because of the shortcomings of legislatures and the weaknesses of political control. According to Patrick Dunleavy (who has himself reformulated and refined the public choice approach to provide an important analysis of the 'Architecture of the British Central State'

(Dunleavy, 1989)), the bureaucratic over-supply model heavily influenced the Thatcher government in the period 1979–82:

> Acting on the assumption that all bureaucracies are wasteful, and spurred on by the premier's hostile reaction to civil service industrial action in 1981, the Conservatives set about cutting Whitehall's manpower and 'deprivileging' the service in pay and pension terms. (Dunleavy, 1986: 363)

Even if, as Dunleavy goes on to point out, government hostility towards Whitehall was subsequently muted, his observation (written in the mid-1980s) that 'ideas for continued radical change were put on a back burner' (*ibid.*) was destined soon to be overtaken by a further tidal wave of reform – beginning with the launching of the Next Steps programme in 1988, which was followed by a major programme of market testing.

Apart from its ideas about bureaucracy, public choice theory also offers a critique of party politics, at least as it operates in local government. To quote Loughlin's succinct summary:

> The theory of politics argues, on the supply side, that political parties, in bidding for support, end up by promising more than they can deliver and that, on the demand side, this leads to inflated expectations since the electorate have incentives to vote for increased services because they do not pay for them directly and because there may be little correlation between tax payments and government benefits. (Loughlin, 1992: 98)

Most New Right analysts (Hayek in particular) are strong believers in the rule of law; though they are generally hostile to the idea that 'constitutions can be designed to conform with their normative goals' (Dunleavy and O'Leary, 1987: 126). However, having identified the economic reasons for the inevitability of government failure, public choice theory offers prescriptions for reform, which amount to calls for variable constitutional constraints upon government action – including limitations upon the scope of taxation, and 'sunshine' laws, which expire after a given period unless renewed. Some of these constitutional ideas are more applicable to a country like America, with a codified constitution, than to the UK, where the scope for entrenchment, in the face of parliamentary sovereignty, the doctrine that no Parliament can bind its successors, is limited.

There have been substantial academic critiques of the public choice position (e.g. Goodin, 1982). But a powerful undercurrent of it remains in recent Conservative politics. There is a strong residual flavour of public choice in the language of the Citizen's Charter, and in the rhetoric of ministers in the 1990s. Thus William Waldegrave, appointed by Major in 1992 to the newly created office of Minister of Public Service and Science, has described the post-war development of public services, in which:

> the interests of the providers systematically outweighed those of the users, and which, driven only by the natural tendency of all provider organisations to claim that they can only do better with more money, contained an overwhelming dynamic for increased cost which was bound to end in conflict with reality. Many loyal public servants did good work within them – but the seeds of their own destruction were firmly embedded in the organisations' structures. (Waldegrave, 1993: 8)

It is notable that this scepticism about party politics has not extended to Parliament and government ministers and that claims have not been made to restrict their activities, by law or in other ways. The preference for non-legal control still prevails in Civil Service reform.

CORE FUNCTIONS OF THE STATE

In November 1992, Stephen Dorrell, then Financial Secretary to the Treasury, told the Centre for Policy Studies (CPS) that the government was:

> initiating a new review of the activities of Government to develop the successful privatisation programme of the last decade. This privatisation initiative involves a 'long march' through Whitehall ... In every department of state, we must apply the 'back to basics' test to every area of government. We are no longer simply looking for obvious candidates for privatisation. The conventional question was 'what can we sell?' That question must now be turned on its head. Now we should ask ourselves 'what must we keep?' What is the inescapable core of government? (Dorrell, 1992)

The inexorable growth of large-scale, interventionist government since the middle of the nineteenth century has been well documented. New Right theory and Thatcherite policy have sought to reduce the functions of government and to 'roll back the frontiers of the state'. To that end, many public functions have been privatized; many of those that remain face market testing, with a view to privatization; public servants have been required to adopt a more businesslike approach to their tasks and to be more sensitive to their customers, as the Citizen's Charter shows (see Chapter 3); and public sector institutions have been required to forge new partnerships with the private and voluntary sectors, and with one another (sometimes, as with the NHS, in the framework of an internal market – albeit, as Metcalfe notes, a 'rigged' one).

Stephen Dorrell's remarks make clear that the government is far from regarding the process as being complete. But where will it end? What are the 'core functions' of the state? Presumably the most fervent New Right ideologue would not take the process back to Adam Smith's view, expressed more than two hundred years ago in *The Wealth of Nations*, that the duties of government should be confined to national defence, law, order and justice, and some basic public works? Ostensibly, the process has already gone a long way: for instance, aspects of prison, police and even defence services have been contracted out. Of course, the 'public' status of a service does not necessarily disappear just because it is exercised by or shared with the private sector (as the extension of the jurisdiction of the PCA to investigate complaints about functions discharged under contract indicates: see Chapter 5).

The applicability of judicial review (see Chapter 5), which can only be applied to issues of public law and to bodies on the fringes of the public sector, is regularly tested in litigation – with varying results. In 1987, in *R. v Panel on Take-overs and Mergers, ex parte Datafin* [1987] QB 815, the Court of Appeal held that the City of London's Panel on Takeovers and Mergers was susceptible to judicial review. Since *Datafin*, however, as David Pannick has observed, the courts have had to deal with applications for judicial review against a wide range of 'private' bodies, and have held that it applies to the decisions of the Advertising Standards Authority and the Code of Practice Committee of the British Pharmaceutical Association, but not to the decisions of the Jockey Club, the Chief Rabbi or the Football Association (Pannick, 1992).

Some of the relationships between service providers are founded on the private law of contract; some are said to rest on quasi-contracts, which may or may not be justiciable. It has been suggested that a new form of public law contract needs to be developed to accommodate the radically altered landscape of public service provision (Harden, 1992).

These, then, are the major themes and theories that have affected public sector reform in the last decade or so. We turn in the next chapter to consider how these ideas have been translated into new techniques and institutional changes in public services.

3

New Public Management: Techniques and Institutional Changes

As we noted in the last chapter, Thatcherism and the public sector reform programme associated with it were not an all-embracing blueprint written by the lone hand of a visionary prime minister in 1979. And the reforms in the Civil Service, local government and the NHS in Britain have been brought in on an incremental basis without any prior master plan or grand design having been developed.

The process bears many similarities to changes that have been taking place in other countries. As we also saw in the last chapter, Osborne and Gaebler (1992) have given the label 'reinventing government' to the eclectic, pluralistic approach that has been applied to public service reform in the United States, a tag which fits quite comfortably much of what is happening in the United Kingdom too (see Lewis, 1993; Butler, 1994; but see also the less positive views of Jordan, 1994; Rhodes, 1994b).

According to this view, the role of governments is 'steering not rowing', empowering communities and not simply delivering services, encouraging competition rather than monopoly, focusing on outcomes rather than inputs, meeting the needs of the 'customer' not the bureaucracy, decentralization of authority, and solving problems by 'leveraging' the market-place, rather than by creating public programmes (Osborne and Gaebler, 1992).

With the benefit of hindsight we can identify three broad techniques in public service reform in the United Kingdom: empowering the consumer, government by contract, and taking the politics out of public service provision. In terms of accountability, the combined effects of these techniques could be summarized as reducing the level of political accountability for services and increasing the use of market mechanisms and consumer power as ways of imposing accountability.

'CHARTERISM': EMPOWERING THE CONSUMER

The Citizen's Charter (1991, Cm 1599) is at the centre of a policy which seeks to give a greater voice to 'consumers' of public services. Steps in this direction had been taken before the charter was published in 1991 (increasing the choice of schools for their children that was available to parents, increasing the say of tenants in the management of local-authority-owned housing, for instance), but the policy was first made explicit across a wide range of public service activity in the charter. The charter is seen as a ten-year programme of radical reform that touches on the relationship between services and their customers and many other aspects of service provision which are less directly the concern of customers – notably the quest for value for money through the 'Competing for Quality' programme launched in November 1991 (Cm 1730); market testing (see *The Government's Guide to Market Testing*, 1993); contracting out; staff savings; deregulation; performance-related pay in the Civil Service; and the removal of Crown immunities.

The Citizen's Charter (1991) was presented to Parliament by the prime minister in July 1991 and was published in the form of a Command Paper. It promised to be 'the big idea' that the Conservatives, like the other parties, were looking for in what was then thought to be the run-up to an imminent general election. Personally backed from the outset by John Major, it can be seen as an important link in the chain of post-1979 public service reform. In particular, as far as the Civil Service is concerned, it has been depicted as a logical progression from the Next Steps initiative. According to Brian Hilton, director of the Citizen's Charter Unit in the Cabinet Office, the Charter was: 'the next stage after Next Steps. Next Steps gets management sorted out and now we are saying with greater clarity what we want management to deliver' (quoted by P. Hennessy, *Independent*, 7 October 1991). The charter has become a prominent feature of the agendas of the Next Steps agencies and of the framework agreements that set out their performance targets. In many ways Next Steps is the vehicle for the delivery of the Citizen's Charter in central government through the agencies which serve the public. It also applies to local government, the NHS, the courts and the police, and it foreshadowed stronger powers for the regulatory agencies: the Competition and Service (Utility) Act 1992 strengthened the powers of the regulators of the privatized telecommunications, gas, electricity supply and water industries.

The Citizen's Charter reaffirmed the government's continuing commitment to privatization, to the further contracting out of public services, and to the extension of compulsory competitive tendering and market testing; but it implicitly accepted that a lot of major services should and would remain within the public sector – though arguing at the same time that they must be more transparent and consumer-sensitive. Its main themes have been:

- *higher standards:* publication, in clear language, of standards of service; tougher, independent inspectorates; a 'charter mark' scheme to identify bodies that abide by the terms of the charter;
- *openness:* elimination of secrecy about organizational arrangements, costs of service, etc.; staff to be identified by name badges;
- *information:* regular publication of information about performance targets and how well they have been met;
- *non-discrimination:* services to be available regardless of race or sex; leaflets to be printed in minority languages where there is a need;
- *responsiveness:* greater sensitivity to consumer needs; customers to be consulted about services provided;
- *grievances:* better machinery for redress of grievances (including, as originally envisaged, a system of local lay adjudicators to deal with minor claims for redress); adequate remedies, including compensation where appropriate.

Traditionally, the redress for grievances about public service was obtainable either through the courts or tribunals if entitlements had been denied, or through resort to the various ombudsmen, such as the PCA, or internal complaints procedures, or through political channels via parliamentary questions or correspondence between a constituent's MP and the minister or department in question. The Citizen's Charter approach has sought to give consumers of public services some of the power and 'rights' – not for the most part legally enforceable rights – that a customer of a privately provided service might have.

While Next Steps agencies are generally concerned with the 'supply' side of government operations and are intended to improve the overall efficiency and effectiveness of public services, normally within existing resources (see below), the Citizen's Charter is concerned for the most part with the position of particular individual consumers of those services, that is with the 'demand' side. The charter has been seen by the government as an evolution of, and therefore intimately linked with, the executive agency approach and the other reforms in the NHS, privatized industries and local government which were introduced in the 1980s.

The introduction to the charter states that it is a 'toolkit' of initiatives and ideas rather than a 'blueprint' which imposes a drab and uniform pattern on every service. It is of the essence of the working of the charter as seen by the government that improvements should be achieved within existing resources, and: 'The Charter programme is about finding better ways of converting the money that can be afforded into even better services' (*Citizen's Charter*, 1991: 6).

The aims of the Citizen's Charter are in many respects very modest. For the most part it does not provide legal remedies should the services in question fail to meet the charter standards. It is a consumers', not a producers', charter and there is very little in it about improving the working conditions of staff in public services. Indeed, it is an explicit message of the charter that public sector workers (such as teachers, nurses and railway workers) can, and indeed should expect to, have tougher working lives, dealing with the complaints and concerns of empowered, better-informed consumer citizens.

Some of the Next Steps agencies (see below and Chapter 7) are covered by the charter: it refers specifically to the Employment Service and the Social Security Benefits Agency, the Land Registry, and the Driving and Vehicle Licensing Authority, among others. Agency charters include the Benefits Agency Customer Charter, the Employment Service Jobseeker's Charter (see Chapter 7) and the Contributions Agency Contributor's and Employer's Charters. More than thirty other agencies have issued charter standard statements which set out in detail the services provided for customers. The framework documents of agencies covered by the Citizen's Charter and their annual performance agreements (see below) set out their responsibilities, and establish performance targets. For the most part these are not individual, but require, for instance, that a percentage of claims are dealt with within a certain number of days of receipt.

Under the charter, organizations other than executive agencies are also given targets and specified performance indicators (such as maximum waiting times for hospital operations). These provide the criteria against which to measure their performance, and the results are published, sometimes in the form of league tables. (It will be remembered that in Chapter 1 the point was made that clear criteria are needed for accountability to be effective.) The focus is on outcomes rather than inputs, and this has been one of the main features of the New Public Management Revolution, described in the last chapter.

Some public services need to be particularly responsive to the needs of individuals, so the setting down of specific general standards can go only part of the way to meet the problem. This was already recognized in the National Health Service and Community Care Act 1990, which imposes duties on local authorities to assess individual need and requires an 'individual care plan' reflecting the individual's wishes, setting out the services available, and naming the person responsible for them. This measure fits in with the spirit of the Citizen's Charter and is cited in the White Paper as an aspect of the charter and social services (1991, Cm 1599: 21).

It is a strong theme of the charter that much more information should be supplied by service providers to consumers of public services and to the public generally. This is already achieved to some extent by the executive agencies through publication of their framework documents, performance agreements, operational plans, etc., which is a requirement normally imposed by administrative direction to the chief executives. The Employment Service and Social Security Benefits Agencies are required to publish their annual reports. In addition, the Audit Commission's reports on local authorities' performance have been published since 1995, and the Audit Commission is given the task of publishing league tables of local authority performance. Local authorities are required by law to publish their responses to the Audit Commission's reports.

Services dealing with the public are required to publish information about their complaints procedures; staff generally have to be identified by name; and the service providers must make available information about entitlements to benefits and services through leaflets, telephone freelines, and sometimes interviews. In the context of Next Steps, the government has published annual reviews of the progress of the initiative, which summarize in easily digestible, if bland, form the achievements of the agencies (*Improving Management in Government – The Next Steps Agencies: Reviews*, 1990, Cm 1261; 1991, Cm 1760; 1992, Cm 2110; 1993, Cm 2430; 1994, Cm 2750, 1995, Cm 3164). These reviews include summaries of how far short of targets some agencies have fallen, together with explanations. They also include key targets for the following year.

Some of the duties to publish information which the government seeks will have to be imposed by legislation. Others may be imposed through administrative arrangements, particularly in central government, where ministers have the power to make such requirements in framework documents. But they are not legally enforceable by, for example, an aggrieved member of the public seeking the information. However, the *Open Government* White Paper (1993) committed the government to producing a code for disclosure of information, to be monitored by the PCA (there is also a minister with responsibility for open government and the Citizen's Charter).

This position may be contrasted with some of the Citizen's Charters outside the Civil Service and central government, for example in schools and the utilities, where, as we shall see later in this chapter, there are to be legally enforceable duties of disclosure. Another aspect of the use of information to improve services is the government's encouragement to service providers to carry out consumer surveys to enable them to obtain information about the responses and wishes of consumers and to make arrangements to meet their needs.

The charter is also committed to improving inspection and audit. It included proposals to reform inspectorates, including the Schools Inspectorate, the Inspectorate of Constabulary, and the Social Services Inspectorate. They are to be independent of the service inspected, and to include lay members so that 'the voice of the individual citizen' can be heard (*Citizen's Charter: Second Report*, 1994, Cm 2540: 4). They are required to be open about their work and findings.

Concern was expressed about the need to counteract any risk of 'capture' of inspectorates by those subject to inspection, and so the charter 'will therefore begin to open up inspectorates to the outside world (p. 4). Lay members are to be appointed to some inspectorates to balance professional views 'by the sound common sense of other members of the public' (p. 4.). Inspectorates' reports have to be published, and these have included 'league tables' of performance. Public comment is invited on reports.

Improved audit is at the very heart of both the Citizen's Charter and the Next Steps agencies initiatives. This is to be done by the use of 'performance indicators' – which takes us back to the importance of specifying clear criteria in order to achieve effective acountability – and here it will clearly be crucial to select appropriate indicators. This has become an art and a science in itself.

The experience of the Employment Service, whose chief executive admitted to the Select Committee for the PCA that an effect of being performance-driven was to produce an ambiguous attitude to 'customers' among his staff, and a defensive attitude to criticisms made by the PCA (see Chapter 7), illustrates how attitudes can be affected by the pressure imposed by audit and the elaboration of performance targets and indicators in a way that can be detrimental to the treatment of the public served by an agency. This raises important questions about the ultimate objectives of the reforms. It is not always clear whether, for example, performance indicators are to be concerned with improving value for money, customer satisfaction or quality, or simply meeting the requirements of ministers, who may not have thought very carefully about their priorities where these are competing.

The Audit Commission produced a paper and a set of indicators in 1994 (*Citizen's Charter Indicators: Charting a Course*) for specific local authority services. Questions in relation to refuse collection included:

- Does the authority provide the containers for household refuse?
- Does it provide wheeled bins for household waste?
- Is household waste collected from the back doors of domestic properties?
- Is garden waste collected?

- Are recyclable materials collected separately from household waste?

Also included were the authority's targets for the reliability of household waste collection services, performance against targets and so on. Information that enables comparisons to be made between authorities is published, thus exposing providers to pressure to improve performance if it falls short of that of comparable authorities.

A particular significance, for our purposes, of the focus on performance indicators, framework documents, operational plans and annual performance agreements is that it indicates a switch away from inputs, processes and procedures to *outputs* and thus to *outcomes* (Eighth Report of the Treasury and Civil Service Committee, 1989–90, *Progress in the Next Steps Initiative*). This is not the sole purpose of the reforms, since the Citizen's Charter is concerned to some degree with process and procedure in the sense that it imposes time limits for dealing with applications, considerate treatment by staff, complaints procedures and the like. But the thrust of the Next Steps reforms is that, very much in the general spirit of the New Public Management, results assume greater importance than hitherto.

The Citizen's Charter seeks to improve the procedures and the substantive remedies for redress of grievances of individual 'customers' of the services covered by the charter in a range of ways, some of them entirely new. The bodies covered by the charter should have and publicize complaints procedures. But the charter also looks at independent complaints machinery. It mentions the PCA and the NHS Commissioners with brief approval, but does not propose to alter their jurisdiction or, for example, allow the bypassing of MPs and direct access. However, the PCA has himself indicated that he will regard failure to meet standards set out in charters as *prima facie* evidence of maladministration if the standards are sufficiently specific (Annual Report 1993: para. 6). The charter does undertake that, should arrangements for the Commissioner for Local Administration not put an end to difficulties in the implementation of recommendations, the government will take the further step of introducing legislation to make the recommendations legally enforceable, on the model of the Northern Ireland Complaints Commissioner.

For some complaints against public services a system of lay adjudicators was promised. Participation in the scheme would have been voluntary. It was not envisaged that these bodies would have coercive powers and the jurisdiction was to be dependent on the agreement of both sides in advance to abide by decisions. Although the general scheme of lay adjudicators never materialized (apparently the Treasury became worried about the costs), since the publication of the Citizen's

Charter a number of appointments of 'complaints adjudicators' have been made: a Revenue and Customs and Excise Adjudicator, who deals directly with complaints about tax and customs and excise matters (not those that raise legal issues); and adjudicators for the Contributions Agency, Companies House and Prisons (to deal with prisoners' complaints). These appointments have not been statutory, though the terms on which the offices have been established give them a degree of independence.

There is no legal obligation on the bodies over which an adjudicator has jurisdiction to give effect to the recommendations of the adjudicators, but access to the PCA (via MPs) will remain open to complainants who are dissatisfied. The Select Committee on the PCA has commended these appointments as a valuable means whereby a department can give adequate consideration to the majority of its complaints, thus helping to reduce the workload of the ombudsman, enabling him or her to concentrate on the more serious and intractable cases (*Fourth Report of the Select Committee on the Parliamentary Commissioner for Administration*, 1994–5, HC 394: para. 22).

In relation to some disputes, especially between utilities and their customers, the Competition and Service (Utilities) Act 1992 gives power to directors general (of telecommunications, gas, electricity supply and water services) to deal with certain disputes with customers, for example by determining compensation for failure to reach the prescribed standard of service, or determining disputes about electricity bills. In other cases the government shies away from the idea of awarding compensation to customers for the service's failure to come up to standards: 'No-one wants money diverted from improving the service or ensuring, if possible, that a mistake is not repeated' (*Citizen's Charter*: 47). Hence, for instance, there is no promise of compensation for NHS patients who have to wait for treatment: instead the district health authority may have to seek provision of treatment elsewhere, if appropriate from the independent sector (*Citizen's Charter*: 47). On the other hand, there are proposals for compensation by way of refund for British Rail passengers in the case of delays or cancellations, or by way of extension to season tickets as compensation for days when there is no effective service (*Citizen's Charter*: 49).

The Citizen's Charter and the Next Steps initiatives both rely on incentives as instruments of policy: performance-related pay is being introduced in executive agencies. The charter introduces a 'charter mark' which is awarded to services that reach certain high standards. By February 1996, sixty-two charter marks had been awarded to executive agencies, some to agencies as a whole (Companies House, the Royal Parks Agency and the UK Passport Agency, for instance) and others to offices within agencies (three district offices of the Employment Service,

HM Customs and Excise Edinburgh VAT Office and HM Prison Bedford Library). The assumption is that agencies and other public bodies will be keen to bring their services up to standard in order to achieve the charter mark, and then to keep them up to scratch in order not to lose it. This seems the modern, governmental version of the 'By Royal Appointment' or 'Kitemark' accolades.

Many public sector bodies have been issuing their own sectoral charters (Parent's Charter, Taxpayer's Charter, etc.). By the end of 1994 some thirty-eight charters had been published and brought into operation, and some of them had been reissued since first publication with revised, higher standards (*Citizen's Charter: Second Report*, 1994, Cm 2540). In May 1996 the total stood at forty.

GOVERNMENT BY CONTRACT

Linked with charterism and the 'consumerization' of public administration has been the progressive introduction of various forms of 'contract' as a management tool in public services since the mid-1980s (Harden, 1992). Local government has been subjected to a compulsory competitive tendering regime, which requires it to put large sections of the work previously performed by its own direct labour organizations (refuse collection and street cleaning, for instance) out to tender in the market. However, direct labour organizations may tender for this work, and many have done so successfully. The technique has driven down labour costs. The contracts specify the level of service (a further example of the use of explicit accountability and performance criteria) and provide for sanctions for failure to reach the required level, so that new methods of 'enforcement' of standards are available to the local authority as contractor.

As already noted, soon after the launch of the Citizen's Charter the government announced a programme of 'market testing' in its White Paper *Competing for Quality* (1991, Cm 1730) for many activities carried out within government, with a view to securing better 'value for money' from the private sector or from its own staff if they were able to compete. This process was followed up by the passage of the Deregulation and Contracting Out Act 1994, which facilitates the contracting out of activities for which ministers are legally responsible.

As an alternative to contracting out, in some services such as the NHS a purchaser/provider split has been introduced. In the NHS 'internal market' this entails 'contractual' negotiations taking place between health authorities or general practitioner fundholders, which purchase services for patients, and hospital trusts, which provide the services to patients. This technique is designed to encourage better cost-effectiveness in the spending of public money. It is also designed to define the standard of service and its cost (thus providing the criteria for accountability), and may be seen as part of the redefinition of the function of the 'reinvented' state, as facilitating and defining, not providing, services.

A 'purchaser/provider' split may also be detected in the Next Steps initiative in the Civil Service (see below): executive agencies operate under negotiated 'framework' documents which in some respects resemble contracts for the supply of the service in question to the minister. This process of contractualization has gone much further in New Zealand (see Chapter 8).

To lawyers the idea of a contract suggests that there are (1) clearly defined obligations between identified parties, and (2) remedies for breach of those obligations, and hence an effective process of legal accountability between the parties for failure to perform the terms of the contract. The doctrine of privity of contract means that only the parties to a contract can normally have rights under it, and that obligations can only arise where 'consideration' has been given for the benefit of the contract: 'voluntary' promises to deliver services, for example, are not enforceable. The use of the notion of a 'contract' in the public service, however, differs from the concept set out above, because these 'contracts' – for example, between executive agencies and ministers, or between health authorities and hospitals – are, for the most part, deliberately not made legally enforceable. Instead, other, non-legal 'remedies' for breach of 'contractual' obligations are provided for – arbitration in the NHS or withholding of performance-related pay in executive agencies, for instance.

Linked to the use of the technique of contract to define relationships and obligations in the public service is the idea that certain bundles of functions and people performing them are separated out (either legally, as in the NHS institutional separation of service purchasers from providers, or organizationally, as in the Civil Service), and treated to a greater or lesser extent as independent, accountable, and having control over their own activities and budgets. Without this sort of separation the 'contract' approach outlined above would obviously not be possible.

Under the White Paper *The Civil Service: Continuity and Change* (1994, Cm 2627), the use of contract as a management tool is to be extended into the 'Senior Civil Service' (Grade 5 and above) from April 1996, with the introduction of explicit, written employment contracts which include 'better, more flexible pay arrangements which recognise increased levels of personal responsibility, reward successful performance' (paras 1.5, 4.32). As we shall see in Chapter 5, where we consider the legal basis for public administration, the idea of the relationship between government and civil servants as one of an employment contract rather than that of the holding of an office with responsibilities to a general public interest is a controversial one.

TAKING THE POLITICS OUT OF PUBLIC SERVICE PROVISION

The third broad technique adopted to improve the efficiency and effectiveness of the public services in the last fifteen years or so has been the depoliticization of the processes of service provision and its control. Until the early 1980s there was a political consensus that, in an electoral, parliamentary democracy, deliverers of services to the public and public servants generally should be accountable, directly or indirectly, through the ballot box to the public.

As we saw in Chapter 1, the constitutional theory went, and still goes, that civil servants are accountable to their ministers, who are accountable in turn to Parliament, which is accountable to the electorate (Woodhouse, 1994); councillors on local authorities are 'responsible' for the work their authorities do and are answerable to their local publics through the ballot box. Where services were delivered through autonomous bodies, there were generally to be included in the membership people who were elected: so police authorities, for instance, counted among their memberships not only magistrates, who are not publicly or politically accountable for what they do save to the extent that it attracts the attention of the press, but also members elected from among the councillors on the relevant local authorities.

There always have been important exceptions to this general constitutional understanding that public bodies should be politically or publicly accountable in some way. Nationalized industries, for instance, never had elected members on their boards; local authority representation was removed from district health authorities in 1991 (though local authorities do nominate half the members of community health councils). But the chairs of nationalized industries were always appointed and could be removed by ministers, and they were subject to ministerial direction on certain strategic matters; the chair of the NHS management executive is a ministerial appointee, as are the chairs of the regional and district health authorities and of NHS trusts.

Since the National Audit Act 1983, many public bodies substantially supported by public funds have been financially accountable through the Comptroller and Auditor General and the National Audit Office to the House of Commons. And since 1977 the Health Service Commissioner (the NHS ombudsman) has been charged with investigating complaints by individuals of maladministration or failures of service leading to injustice; he or she is responsible to Parliament for his or her work. So there is some kind of a line of political accountability for the actions of many bodies operating outside the Civil Service or local government and therefore outside the traditional mechanisms of political and public accountability (see Weir and Hall, 1994).

In addition, all bodies discharging public or governmental functions are subject to the law of the land and in particular to judicial review (see Chapter 5), a non-political form of accountability. The development of techniques of audit, backed up generally by political accountability through the Public Accounts Committee (PAC) of the House of Commons or departmental and Treasury pressures, is another example of a form of accountability that is not directly political (see Power, 1994; White *et al.*, 1994; Audit Commission, 1994).

Since the early 1980s there has been an increasing loss of confidence in the efficacy of political accountability in securing good administration, indeed a perception, certainly in respect of local government, that political accountability and the legitimacy of political involvement in public service delivery that accountability brought about might undermine the efficacy of service delivery. We could take this as an example of the relationship between responsibility and accountability discussed earlier: if a minister is accountable to Parliament for what happens in his or her department and decisions taken in his or her name, then the assumption might be that he or she is entitled to intervene in operational decision making in those areas, to the possible detriment of efficiency and effectiveness; similarly, if local councillors are accountable for the decisions of their authorities, they would expect to be entitled to make operational decisions.

In other words, they could slip from accountability to 'responsibility' in the sense of personally taking on the operational jobs to be done. In local government in particular, the perception has grown on the part of Conservative governments that if councillors are in a position to take political decisions on operational matters, to intervene in the day-to-day running of services, they may impede the efficacy of the operations concerned. Local authorities were also considered to be over-politicized in those areas where strategic rather than operational decisions fell to be made. This perception has resulted in the progressive removal from local authorities of many of their functions, and the depoliticization of other areas of local government activity. The independent tax base of local government, the domestic rates, was first closely controlled by 'capping' and then abolished and replaced by a community charge and then the council tax. The proportion of local authority income raised from the council tax has been greatly reduced, and a higher proportion now comes from central government, with increased central control over how those resources may be spent. The business rate is now centrally fixed and collected by government and distributed on a formula basis to local authorities, so they have lost entirely this independent source of revenue.

The freedom of action of local authorities has been greatly reduced as a result. The housing budget is 'ring fenced'. Schools previously directly run by local education authorities now run their budgets independently under the local management of schools (LMS) arrangement. Much local authority housing has been either sold to tenants or transferred to housing associations. The former polytechnics, now universities, obtained corporate status independent of the local authorities that formerly owned and ran them.

An assumption behind such initiatives has been that elected councillors had been subject to 'capture' by political parties and vested interests such as local government trade unions – a version of 'public choice' theory (see Chapter 3) – to the detriment of the services they were providing and the public they were supposed to be serving. The view developed that consumers of services can and should be involved in many aspects of the running of public services, especially schools (the biggest of all traditional local government services); consumers – in school education, parents and prospective employers of school leavers – can and would better promote the 'consumer' interest in public administration, the 'demand side' of things; increased opportunities for parental choice as to the school their children were sent to would also serve to promote the consumer interest in education. This set of ideas linked in with the Citizen's Charter and New Public Management theory that people from non-political, business or professional – i.e. managerial – backgrounds, with their experience of and commitment to maximizing output gained from working in business, have particularly valuable contributions to make to the delivery of public services (see Chapter 3).

In central government too there has been a degree of depoliticization of activity as a result of the use of agency status for operations within departments (see below). As we noted in Chapter 1, the degree to which ministers regard themselves as 'responsible' for what happens in these bodies is a matter of controversy, and their ability to intervene on a day-to-day basis has been quite deliberately diminished by the introduction of Next Steps agencies (see below and Chapter 7).

While there has been a process of depoliticization in many areas of public administration, in other areas there has been a centralizing trend, which can run counter to the depoliticization process. This is particularly the case in respect of schools, which are encouraged to opt out of local government control in order to become directly funded by the Department for Education (DFE) via its funding agency. Potentially, this could lead to increasing central government intervention (opponents of the policy see it as 'meddling') in these schools. The introduction of the National Curriculum for schools has placed very considerable control over what is taught in schools in the hands of the Secretary of State for Education. And the use of quangos (such as the Higher Education Funding Councils for England, Wales, Scotland and Northern Ireland, and many others) has increased the political input of the ministers who make appointments to them, and who are not required to secure parliamentary approval for such appointments (*First Report of the Committee on Standards in Public Life*, 1995; Weir and Hall, 1994).

INSTITUTIONAL REFORMS IN THE PUBLIC SERVICES

Our brief survey of the techniques of consumerization, contractualization and depoliticization in public services has hinted at some of the institutional reforms that have been introduced in the Civil Service, local government and the NHS in the period with which we are concerned.

Contractualization requires 'corporatization', separating out purchasing and providing organizations, either as a matter of the internal arrangements within an institution, or more formally by granting separate corporate legal identity to the bodies. For this reason both formal and informal arrangements for corporatization have been adopted. Polytechnics obtained formal legal corporate status quite independent of local authorities before their links with local authorities were completely broken by changes in funding. In the NHS there has been a formal legal separation between health authorities, which purchase services, and hospital trusts, which provide them. By contrast, within the Civil Service the separation between purchaser and provider (which is essential to the working of the Next Steps initiative) has been an internal administrative one only, with the result that the 'contracts' between the department and the agency are only 'quasi-contracts' and 'corporatization' is, by the same token, only 'quasi-corporatization', in these arrangements.

THE FINANCIAL MANAGEMENT INITIATIVE AND NEXT STEPS

Since the late 1970s, what could well be regarded as 'a revolution in Whitehall' has taken place. From 1973, government activity could be carried on on a trading-fund basis (i.e. in a manner analagous to the financial accounting arrangements for private sector companies), and by April 1995 twelve agencies were operating as trading funds. Then, a series of procedures was introduced that was designed to improve financial management and coordination in the service. The Financial

Management Initiative (FMI) of 1982 (Cmnd 8616) sought to continue the process of transforming civil servants where appropriate from administrators to managers by devolving more responsibility for departmental budgets to specific civil servants. 'Rayner reviews' of departmental efficiency were introduced in the 1980s, and subjected particular areas of activity to scrutiny with a view to the making of efficiency savings. The National Audit Act of 1983 sought to improve the economy and value for money of the service by subjecting it to enhanced audit procedures.

In 1988 a logical 'next step' was taken in the reform of those aspects of Civil Service activity which are concerned with service delivery. A team within the prime minister's Efficiency Unit produced a report, *Improving Management in Government: The Next Steps*, which proposed the setting up of quasi-autonomous 'executive agencies' within the Civil Service. The proposals were accepted by the government in principle, the plans were spelt out in greater detail in a White Paper on *The Financing and Accountability of Next Steps Agencies* (1989, Cm 914), and an office was established within the Cabinet Office, charged with implementing the programme. By April 1996 there were 125 agencies (plus the Executive Units and offices of the revenue departments), covering 71 per cent of the Civil Service and employing over 382,000 civil servants.

It should be noted, in passing, that the idea of departmental agencies as such was nothing new: several important agencies, such as the Property Services Agency and the Manpower Services Commission, long pre-date the Next Steps programme. It must also be made clear that Next Steps agencies are not the same thing as 'quangos'. The latter – the name popularly given to what the government calls non-departmental public bodies (see McEldowney 1994b: 133–4; Nolan Report, 1995, Cm 2850; Ch. 4) – usually operate on a statutory basis. There are numerous quangos performing a wide variety of executive, advisory and (if one includes administrative tribunals) judicial functions: among the best known are the Equal Opportunities Commission, the Gaming Board, the Arts Council, the Higher Education Funding Council, the Legal Aid Board and the Monopolies and Mergers Commission: 'such bodies have a role in the process of national government but are not part of a department and operate at arms' length from Ministers' (McEldowney, 1994b: 133).

Quangos thus have a legal and constitutional status that is quite different from that of Next Steps agencies. It has been suggested that the affirmation by Margaret Thatcher – who had, soon after becoming prime minister, launched a crusade against the proliferation and non-accountability of quangos – that the new agencies would remain within the Civil Service and subject to ministerial responsibility may have been motivated in part by her anxiety to avoid the appearance of a U-turn (Pliatzky, 1992).

Under the Next Steps arrangements, activities carried on within departments that are thought suitable for agency status are identified, and a 'framework document' is then drawn up after negotiations between the department – in practice the permanent secretary and the minister – and a chief executive, appointed with responsibility for those activities. Chief executive posts are normally advertised, so that applications can be considered from within the Civil Service and from outside; as a result, many applicants have had local government or private sector experience. Of the 113 chief executives and chief executives designate appointed by April 1995, seventy-one had been recruited by open competition, of whom thirty-five had come from outside the Civil Service.

The framework document (yet another instance of the use of explicit criteria to promote accountability and responsibility) defines the functions of the agency and the policy that it is to pursue, and sets targets for performance. By way of example, the framework document for the Employment Service (see Chapter 7) is some twelve well-spaced pages in length, and describes briefly the status, aim and objectives of the agency, the responsibilities of the secretary of state, the chief executive and the permanent secretary, and the delegation of authority to the chief executive. It sets out the understandings about accountability to Parliament, and deals with financial and planning control, services and organization, pay and personnel matters, and arrangements for review of the framework document and modification of it. Once the framework document is finalized, the chief executive is responsible for its implementation, and the performance-related element of his or her salary reflects this responsibility.

By April 1994, twenty-one agencies plus the two revenue departments (the Inland Revenue and Customs and Excise) and the Health and Safety Executive had taken on delegated responsibility for their own pay and pay-related conditions of service – about 60 per cent of the staff in the home Civil Service. All remaining agencies employing over 500 staff had been invited to put forward proposals for their pay and pay-related conditions of service by 1 April 1995, and this policy in relation to staff below senior levels is to be extended to all departments.

Framework documents will normally stand for three years or so, after which they may be reviewed and renegotiated. But it is possible for this to happen at any time, so that on a change of government it will be open to the new administration to set different priorities and targets for the agency: it is for this reason that the arrangements have been described as 'transferable technology' by one commentator (TCSC, 1990). Each year an annual performance agreement is negotiated between the chief

41

executive and the department, setting out targets in more detail. Although the formal provisions for agencies do not require an advisory board or anything of the kind (cf. the Swedish position: see Chapter 8), in practice each agency has such a board or group, though some have non-executive directors or departmental groups (see Chapter 7).

For the most part these arrangements have been introduced by administrative fiat within departments and without the need for legislation or formality (see Chapter 5). However, the Government Trading Act 1990 expanded the power of ministers to set up large parts of the Civil Service on company lines (for instance, Her Majesty's Stationery Office (HMSO) and the Vehicle Inspectorate: see Chapter 7); and chief executives have been appointed as 'agency accounting officers'. The Next Steps model is highly flexible, so that the range of arrangements can be tailored to the needs of particular functions. Like the Citizen's Charter, it is a 'toolkit' rather than a 'blueprint'.

As far as accountability is concerned, in theory the established conventions of ministerial responsibility continue to apply: chief executives are civil servants, they are accountable to the minister, and the minister is accountable to Parliament. But the Next Steps arrangements have resulted in changes in the procedure for dealing with parliamentary questions and MPs' correspondence (see Chapter 6). Under traditional arrangements, parliamentary questions were always answered by the minister to whom they were directed. In practice of course the matter would have been passed down the line to the appropriate Civil Service level in the department, investigation made and a response passed back to the minister. Where letters to ministers from MPs or written parliamentary questions concern executive agency activity, the position now is that such questions on operational matters within the ambit of an executive agency are referred in the first instance to the agency chief executive and his or her answers are published, with his or her name attached, in the Official Report (Hansard). Ministers continue to answer written questions which raise policy issues, and all oral questions.

The TCSC has supported these arrangements in principle, but considers that:

> it remains important that Ministers maintain an engagement
> with individual cases raised by way of Parliamentary questions
> ... We believe that Ministerial intervention will sometimes be
> desirable, particularly in individual cases, and is a necessary part
> of a Minister's role. Ministers should always respond where
> Members of Parliament consider the response by an Agency
> Chief Executive to be unsatisfactory. (TCSC 1993–4, Fifth

Report, *The Role of the Civil Service*, HC 27: para. 170; see also Evans, 1995)

Here we have a reassertion by the House of Commons of ministerial responsibility, in the sense that a minister has a job to do, and should take the blame if it is not done well. The select committees have also been pressing for chief executives to be directly accountable to Parliament – as is the case already with accounting officers (though, as already noted, chief executives have become the accounting officers for their agencies).

The establishment of Next Steps agencies has not been the end of the story of public sector reform by any means. The government and the TCSC have found in these reforms a stimulus to considering what the 'irreducible core' (see Chapter 2) of the Civil Service might be. The government pursued the possibilities in this direction with its market testing programme from 1991 (1991, Cm 1730, *Competing for Quality*; 1993, *The Government's Guide to Market Testing*) and the Deregulation and Contracting Out Act 1994, which provides for the contracting out of functions formerly the responsibility of ministers.

In *The Civil Service: Continuity and Change* (1994, Cm 2627) and *The Civil Service: Taking Forward Continuity and Change* (1995, Cm 2748), the government proposes that departments and agencies should have greater freedom and flexibility to develop programmes for improving efficiency, including ones concerning matters of pay and grading. The so-called 'prior options' policy (*Continuity and Change*, 1994: Ch. 2; *Taking Forward Continuity and Change*, 1995: para. 3.7) requires departments to consider whether a function needs to be done at all, and if so, whether it is a job for which the government should take responsibility. If the answer to this question is 'yes', then consideration must be given to whether the function should actually be carried out by the government, or by some other body. As already noted, members of the 'Senior Civil Service' are to be employed on explicit written employment contracts.

This completes our brief introductory survey of the techniques and institutional reforms that have been introduced in the provision of public services with a view to improving economy, efficiency and effectiveness in the last fifteen years or so. In the next chapter we review some of the principles and problems associated with reform, before turning, in Chapter 5, to the role – in practice, as we shall see, a surprisingly limited role – of the law in public management and administration.

4

The Public Sector Reforms: Principles and Problems

Public sector and public service reform has been near the top of the agenda of public policy in Britain for nearly twenty years, and has been the subject of sharp divisions between the main political parties. These divisions have, it is true, become somewhat less marked, in particular as the Labour Party has moved away from the long-standing commitment, in Clause 4 of its original constitution (abandoned in 1995 as part of Tony Blair's campaign to modernize the party), to wholesale public ownership and towards explicit acceptance of the virtues of a mixed economy in which 'undertakings essential to the common good are either owned by the public or accountable to them' (to cite the new Clause 4). Innovations such as Next Steps and the Citizen's Charter enjoy cross-party support (albeit with some reservations in detail and emphasis). Early Labour threats to reverse most of the Thatcher government's privatization measures have long been abandoned.

But important political differences remain, in particular in areas of health and social policy, and with reference to the future role of local government and to issues of constitutional and electoral reform. The opposition parties have also on many occasions been critical of the Conservative government in matters to do with regulation, patronage and accountability – some aspects of which we discuss in this chapter and elsewhere in this book.

THE POLITICAL CONTEXT

This is not a book about politics, still less is it a partisan polemic for or against the New Public Management reform agenda. But it is important to bear in mind that the reforms we have been discussing have been driven by *political* forces, and that the identification of any aspects

44

of those reforms as a 'problem' may invite a political response. Politics is very much a matter of drawing up balance sheets, with a lot of value judgements and partisan self-interest thrown in, and arriving at a calculation of what best serves both party and public interest (the latter may or may not always coincide, but politicians tend to assume, or pretend, that they do). Different political parties attach different weights to different variables, and have different values, priorities and interests. So, if we were to suggest, for instance, that recent reforms have attached 'too much' importance to saving costs and 'not enough' to maintaining the quality of service, we would be taking sides on issues at the heart of current party political debate – and that is not our purpose.

This chapter is concerned with second-order political questions: not taking a view about the rights and wrongs of reform as such, but identifying some of the issues and problems that have emerged. We do not pretend, however, that these questions, and our decision to discuss them in a chapter about 'problems', are devoid of any political content.

It should also be noted that the issues addressed here are difficult to test empirically. We can, for instance, identify some potential demarcation problems in deciding who is responsible for different aspects of the success or failure of Next Steps agencies, and give some examples which seem to confirm that such problems have from time to time actually manifested themselves; but we must be cautious about generalizing from particular instances. For one thing, many of the reforms discussed in this book are quite new, and their constitutional implications are not yet clear.

Much of this chapter has to do with the consequences of two inter-related things, both of them aspects of the New Public Management Revolution. First is the 'privatization' (using that word in its broadest sense, to include matters like contracting out services and allowing schools to opt out of local authority control) of state functions, and the consequent growth of the grey area inhabited by quasi-government bodies, agencies, and private and voluntary sector bodies performing a variety of public functions. Such bodies have a wide range of different relationships with the public sector and with one another. Privatization may be said to have an even broader meaning, involving the introduction of private sector management techniques and values into the traditional public service.

Second is the decentralization and diversification of the core public sector, and the consequent 'hollowing out' of the central state (Rhodes, 1994a). These two phenomena have given rise to concern – some of which we have already discussed, or touched upon, in earlier chapters – about such issues as accountability, politicization, nepotism, weakening of corporate culture and collective memory, and a possible slippage of ethical standards. Such concerns are well summarized by Alan Doig:

> The speed and direction of devolved managerial autonomy, together with the promotion of an entrepreneurial culture and of privatisation as a goal for public sector organisations, have raised questions about the vulnerability of public sector organisations, the weakening of the public sector ethos, the impact of private sector perspectives within a public sector context, the consequence of change as parts of an organisation change in different ways at different times, the inevitable balance between public service and personal benefit and the implications of change on existing but ill-defined relationships of accountability, monitoring and control. (Doig, 1995: 207)

But although the issues addressed here are currently very topical, they are not particularly new. They are variants of long-standing concerns, long pre-dating the Thatcher–Major years, and reflect, among other things, the uncodified basis of the British Constitution, and the anti-legalistic culture of public administration.

It is with the topical issue of standards and values in the changing public service that we begin.

STANDARDS AND VALUES

The issue of standards of conduct in public life has emerged in several contexts in the 1990s, culminating in the Nolan and Scott Reports of 1995.

We will see later, in Chapter 6, how aspects of it came to the surface in the 1993–4 inquiry by the House of Commons TCSC into the role of the Civil Service (TCSC, 1993, 1994), which considered, among other things, whether the professional codes relating to the Civil Service need to be reinforced, codified and perhaps put onto a statutory basis. In January 1994, the Commons PAC published a report on the Proper Conduct of Public Business giving several instances of serious financial malpractice in central and local government, and in the NHS (PAC, 1994). The *First Report of the Committee on Standards in Public Life* (1995) endorsed the need for a code for civil servants, and the articulation of ethical principles and rules for ministers. The inquiry conducted by Sir Richard Scott into the Matrix Churchill affair has raised major questions about the conduct of ministers and civil servants in the context of a much-criticized decision to bring criminal proceedings against a company for exporting arms to Iraq, when the government itself had known about and condoned the transactions in question (Scott, 1996); and the Pergau Dam controversy raised some moral as well as legal questions about 'arms for aid' (Foreign Affairs Committee, 1994; PAC, 1994).

The turbulence produced by the cumulative effects of reform across every part of the public sector is undoubtedly the cause of many of these concerns about the ethics and standards of conduct in government. We will see later (Chapter 8) how such concern is echoed in relation to New Zealand, where the fragmentation of the public service means that the tradition of 'statecraft' may be lost. There a code has been part of the chosen solutions to the problem.

But another important contributory factor in the UK has been the longevity of one-party government. Responsible government has to do with the awareness of elected ministers that their shortcomings may result in their losing the next general election. When the electoral pendulum gets stuck, ministers may become careless about standards. Moreover, the political neutrality of the Civil Service may become corroded by a long period of continuous one-party rule.

Parliamentary accountability suffers, too. Opposition parties may become both dispirited in their task as watchdogs and, after a while, so divorced from experience of office that they lose any first-hand insight into the day-to-day realities of government, and the mistakes and misdemeanours that can occur.

NEXT STEPS: A DIVIDED CIVIL SERVICE

We have seen that the Next Steps programme distinguished between two main types of Civil Service function: the traditional 'higher Civil Service' functions of ministerial support and policy making on the one hand, and the 'agency' functions of service delivery on the other. The various issues to do with ethics, standards of conduct and accountability can be addressed at two levels, roughly corresponding to this bifurcation of Civil Service functions.

First, there are issues concerning the working relationships between the higher Civil Service and ministers. These issues relate at one level to the professional values of a service which has traditionally been characterized as 'generalist' (and which the Fulton Report (1968) stigmatized as 'amateur'); but they also go much deeper, to the heart of the British Constitution – which is an uncodified entity, resting largely upon conventions. As will be explained in the next chapter, the Civil Service itself is still administered largely by recourse to that antique device, the royal prerogative. The constitutional tensions arising out of the New Public Management Revolution have given fresh currency to Sidney

Low's famous comment that: 'We live under a system of tacit under-standings. But the understandings themselves are not always under-stood' (Low, 1904: 12).

There have been recent calls for the present motley assortment of rules of Civil Service practice and conduct – whose uncodified character is defended by ministers and top civil servants as being conducive to 'flexibility' – to be put onto a more formal footing. As we will see later, at the beginning of 1995 the government abandoned its long-standing resistance to the promulgation of a Civil Service code, albeit on a non-statutory basis and a code was introduced in 1996.

Second, we need to look at the 'service delivery' end of the Civil Service: at the increasing commercialism and managerialism of public service management. We have already discussed the transfer of many of these functions to Next Steps agencies: in Chapter 7, we will look in some detail at the operation of three of those agencies. In this context, we are looking at the nuts and bolts of the administrative process rather than at the interface between ministers and their advisers (though some agency chief executives do have an important part to play in the policy-making process) and, in so far as legal issues are involved, mainly at administrative law rather than constitutional law (though they are interrelated).

This two-level division – analogous to the classical 'policy–administration' dichotomy, much discussed by writers on public ad-ministration, and equally problematical (Campbell and Peters, 1988) – is artificial, and there is a good deal of overlap. For instance, at a very high level of generality, ethical fundamentals, such as respect for the rule of law and insistence upon financial honesty, are applicable, *mutatis mutandis*, throughout the public service – not just the Civil Service – and at all levels. Similarly, the importation into Whitehall in recent years of business management ideas and private sector advisers has had an impact throughout the Civil Service.

A crucial problem in this context is one of exercising effective accountability and control over public services: services that have been increasingly contractorized and functionally decentralized and frag-mented; services whose day-to-day management is entrusted to non-elected executives operating at arm's length from ministers.

Problems of public sector accountability are not peculiar to Britain, but they manifest themselves in an acute form in a country where there is no codified constitution and very little administrative law, and where ministerial accountability to Parliament, even of ministers in charge of 'old-style' government departments, is of considerable theoretical im-portance but of very limited effectiveness. And the issue takes on a new dimension with the prospect that some agency functions may in due course be privatized.

A FRAGMENTED CIVIL SERVICE

The increasing fragmentation of the Civil Service is a particularly significant issue in this context. Arrangements relating to Civil Service pay and conditions of service have been increasingly decentralized under the Next Steps programme, a process facilitated by the Civil Service (Management Functions) Act 1992, which we discuss in Chapter 5. By April 1994, all agencies with 2000 or more staff were required to be ready to implement their own pay and grading structures, and this requirement has been extended. It has been suggested that market testing, widely applied, would result 'in the dismemberment of anything resembling a large scale Civil Service' (Fry, 1993: 18).

Lord Bancroft, a former head of the Civil Service, and his former deputy Sir John Herbecq – both forced into early retirement in 1981 when Thatcher decided to axe the Civil Service Department – wrote to *The Times* (25 February 1994) expressing concern about the long-term effects upon the efficiency and integrity of public administration, and the weakening of accountability, consequent upon 'the accelerating break-up of the home Civil Service'. They conceded that 'with the ever-growing pervasiveness of central government, ways should be sought to limit the burden of responsibility on ministers and to devise new methods, such as market testing, of enhancing efficiency'. But they warned that:

> this should not be carried to the point at which standards of
> service, of conduct and accountability are put at serious risk ...
> The permanent Civil Service of the State is self-descriptive: it
> has no autonomous existence, it is there to serve the State. If the
> fastidiousness of all its standards is perceived to decline, all
> citizens are diminished.

CORE VALUES OF THE CIVIL SERVICE

The continental administrator is, in general, 'a lawyer, specialising in that branch of law – namely administrative law – which is mostly concerned with the functions of government' (Sisson, 1959: 39). The British administrator, manifestly, is not. United Kingdom government is characterized by the absence of both a codified constitution and the restraining hand of a constitutional court (though the EC treaties, enforced both by the European Court of Justice and by the domestic courts, have developed into a formidable quasi-constitutional restraint). And UK public administration is characterized by the lack of a developed system of administrative law – an enduring characteristic, notwithstanding some important developments in recent years. The regulation of the Civil Service itself is, as we explain in the next chapter, largely a matter of ministerial fiat under the royal prerogative: there is no comprehensive Civil Service Act.

What then are the principles and values upon which the Civil Service is founded? The answer to this question depends upon what part of the Civil Service one is talking about. We can venture some generalizations; for instance, that all civil servants are bound by the law of the land – that is, the ordinary criminal law (including laws that apply with particular force in the public sector, such as those on corruption and official secrecy); civil liability in private law fields of tort and contract (and the latter is potentially of growing importance given the continuing development of a 'contract state', as noted in Chapter 1; see Harden, 1992); and the public law discipline of judicial review (whose substantive rules are almost entirely judge-made, and require officials to observe basic principles of fairness). But even this broadly stated proposition requires recognition that the extent to which the law actually impinges upon the working lives of particular civil servants varies enormously.

The textbooks (and successive heads of the Civil Service, including Sir Robin Butler: see Chapter 6) have reminded us that senior civil servants are obliged to be objective and politically neutral, and owe an over-riding duty to the government of the day. But these rules are much less relevant at lower-grade levels, where officials deliver public services and have little to do with ministers (though ministers remain theoretically 'responsible' for what they do). Particular rules – such as those restricting civil servants' participation in party politics – become less and less strict as we move further away from core departmental activities.

On the other hand, in Next Steps executive agencies there is more emphasis upon standards of service to the public. The supervisory role of the ombudsman becomes more relevant, and the Citizen's Charter (see below) seeks to define and improve standards of service.

In other parts of the Civil Service, specialists, like lawyers and medics, have their own professional codes. These may sometimes be in conflict with other requirements of the job, or with the wishes of ministers. Some of the cross-pressures (the interests of justice and a respect for a fair trial versus the political interests of ministers) that afflict government lawyers have been highlighted by the Matrix Churchill affair (Scott, 1996).

The problem of identifying core values is compounded by the increasing fragmentation of the Civil Service, which makes it hard to locate where the 'core' is to be found, and by the fact that standards of behaviour are by no means static. And of course different individuals will have different perceptions (affected by their own personal standards), and the definition of key terms such as 'values' and 'standards' may be differently understood. Some observers may think in terms of individual morality (e.g. honesty, incorruptibility, sexual propriety), while others may emphasize professional and perhaps constitutional aspects (e.g. political neutrality, obedience to ministerial instructions): though of course these may overlap ('whistleblowing' may be charged as a breach both of the Official Secrets Act and of rules of Civil Service conduct – and defended by claims of higher moral duty towards the public interest). Let us look at a selection of opinions, ancient and modern.

CIVIL SERVICE VALUES AND PUBLIC SECTOR REFORM

Discussing, in the context of a study of the post-Second World War Civil Service, the various reforms that took place in the nineteenth-century Civil Service, Greaves observed that:

> At the time, however, reform succeeded because it suited actual
> needs as they were understood. And these needs were, in the
> main, impeccable honesty, scrupulous administration of the law
> without any uncomfortable disposition to make searching
> inquiry into its social justification, and, at least at the higher
> levels, a social compatibility with ministers. (Greaves, 1947: 10)

The aim underlying the reforms 'was to prevent the waste of public funds and to abolish patronage and corruption. They were designed to establish honesty and efficiency and equality before the law as the basis of the public service' (*ibid.*: 14).

But while there may have been clear ethical principles implicit in such aims, it was by no means self-evident that such values needed to be spelt out in a code. For one thing, although the Northcote Trevelyan Report of 1854 laid down standards for the recruitment of civil servants, the gentlemanly amateurism upon which the post-Northcote Trevelyan Civil Service (or at least the higher Civil Service, giving policy advice to ministers) was based had little place for the formalized ethical statements associated with traditional 'professions', such as law or medicine. For another, the duties of civil servants were (and are) a function of their constitutional relationship with ministers. What would be the status and function of a formal code of Civil Service conduct and ethics when the British Constitution itself is, for better and for worse, uncodified? As will be described in Chapter 6, the issue has been addressed by the Commons TCSC, and the government has introduced a code very similar to that recommended by that committee (HC Deb., vol. 267, col. 234, 23 November 1995). But we have also observed that its legal and constitutional status remains unclear.

THE CIVIL SERVICE AND THE CITIZEN'S CHARTER: RAISING WHAT 'STANDARD'?

At the increasingly fragmented and decentralized service-delivery end of the Civil Service – a long way from ministers and the heartland of the British Constitution – we find a commercialized-consumerist culture, in which standards are defined by reference to perceived best practice in the private sector. It should be noted, however, that the organizational and functional diversity of service-delivery agencies militates against the adoption of any single managerial blueprint and against the emergence of a monolithic culture; some agencies are far more in contact with the public and/or more 'commercial' than others.

Some critics of the New Public Management have expressed scepticism about whether the business-management models that have driven the New Public Management Revolution have always been appropriate (see for instance Stewart and Walsh, 1992; Metcalfe, 1993). There is also a wider and more difficult issue here of whether importing the commercialism of the private sector into the Civil Service significantly threatens to contaminate some of the best traditions of 'public service'. Concerns are sometimes expressed that an obsessive pursuit of performance targets and budgetary stringency may encourage public sector managers to cut corners (perhaps illegally) and public sector workers to forget their duty to the public (as with the example of the time-fixated bus driver, cited in Chapter 6, and the Employment Service's reaction to criticism from the PCA, considered in Chapter 7); that an emphasis on cutting waste may result in the elimination of safeguards such as the double-checking of actions and decisions; and that distancing agencies from central (and ultimately parliamentary) discipline may mean that bad practice is not detected until too late, if at all. This reinforces the case for developing alternative modes of accountability and new variants of public law – a recurrent theme of this book, and one to which we return in the next chapter, and in the concluding chapter.

However, it would be a mistake to accept uncritically either the popular characterization of the business world as inherently amoral and/ or unethical (for instance, many private sector organizations have developed their own codes of ethics) or the New Right dogma that public sector management is inherently less efficient than market-driven management.

The most explicit manifestation of the Major government's preoccupation with consumer satisfaction and standards is the Citizen's Charter, discussed in Chapter 3. The aspect of the charter referring to redress of grievances is particularly important, in that it hints at a new approach to accountability in which administrative law might displace traditional parliamentary forms of accountability. The first step identified by the architects of the charter is to overhaul the public services' own complaints schemes. The criteria set out in the first annual report on the charter (Charter Report, 1992) said that good complaints systems should be effective, readily accessible, simple to operate, speedy, objective, confidential, and integrated with the organization's management information systems.

This last point was emphasized in evidence given by the Charter Unit to the Select Committee on the Parliamentary Commissioner for Administration. As the Director of the Unit, Brian Hilton, put it: 'There is no point in having a complaints group off in the wide blue yonder somewhere; it has to be an integral part.' Citing the example of the new complaints division in Customs and Excise, he said that one of the main jobs of that division 'is not only to ensure that complaints are dealt with, but that they are fed back through to the management so that the appropriate changes needed can be made to cut down the number of complaints in the future' (PCA Committee, 1992: Q. 55).

There is now a complaints task force (headed by Lady Wilcox, Chair of the National Consumer Council) to look at whether public services are in line with these principles, and to advise on setting up and improving complaints systems. It also promised a telephone helpline – Charterline – to give information and advice, including advice about other sources of help, such as the various ombudsmen. In February 1993 it was announced that Charterline was to be piloted in Nottinghamshire, Derbyshire and Leicestershire. However, the experiment did not generate enough public interest to make it worth pursuing further.

To take one instance of a new complaints initiative in the context of the charter: as we saw in Chapters 1 and 3, following the launch of the Taxpayer's Charter in 1991, a Revenue Adjudicator was appointed to investigate taxpayers' complaints. This coincided with the publication of a set of three new codes of practice, setting out standards of performance, and promising compensation for delays or mistakes on the part of the Revenue. The adjudicator considers problems concerning 'excessive delays, errors, discourtesy or the way in which the Revenue has exercised discretion'. Disputes about matters of legal interpretation and tax liability continue to be dealt with by the Income Tax Commissioners and the courts.

The new procedure is intended to complement rather than to supersede existing machinery for redress. The Inland Revenue has over the years been one of the biggest sources of customers for the PCA, accounting on average for around one-sixth of his or her annual caseload. It will still be open to complainants to go (via their MP) to the PCA. Since the appointment of the Revenue Adjudicator a number of similar appointments have been made to other bodies operating on agency lines (including Customs and Excise, the Contributions Agency and Companies House) and the Select Committee on the PCA has endorsed such appointments.

There was some discussion in the PCA Select Committee's Report about the possibility that improvements in internal complaints procedures might diminish the workload of the PCA. The Committee agreed that this would be 'beneficial', but regarded it as 'essential to retain an external, impartial investigator such as the Parliamentary Commissioner for Administration' (PCA Committee, 1992: para. 7). It should perhaps be a matter for concern that the proliferation of in-service complaints mechanisms, as promised by the charter, and of complaints adjudicators may result in the further, and damaging, fragmentation of an already fragmented system.

Those who see the charter as signalling a new dawn of administrative law are probably doomed to disappointment. The charter itself is not a justiciable document. And William Waldegrave, Minister of Public Service and Science, true to the British tradition of regarding law and lawyers as impediments rather than as aids to good government, told the TCSC, with reference to the new redress systems promised by the charter, that 'if we can avoid getting too many lawyers involved in these redress systems, except when issues are very, very serious, so much the better I think' (TCSC, 1993: Q. 27).

THE ACCOUNTABILITY OF CIVIL SERVANTS TO PARLIAMENT

It has been increasingly recognized in Britain in recent years that civil servants need to become much more accountable in their own right. Hence the increased propensity (noted in Chapter 6) for select committees to take evidence from civil servants; and hence the development of a UK ombudsman system. The Next Steps programme makes agency chief executives accounting officers for their agencies, and generally they are answerable for 'operational' (as distinct from 'policy', though in practice the distinction is far from clear-cut) and financial matters. In some cases chief executives do have a role in giving policy advice – the Prisons Service and the Employment Service (see Chapter 7) are examples. The accountability of officials running and working in agencies and other public bodies is enhanced by the 'empowerment' of the consumers of public services (the Citizen's Charter is the clearest manifestation of this) and by modest moves to make government more open and transparent.

Yet even changes which implicitly recognize the limitations of ministerial responsibility still cling on to it. The PCA (unlike his or her Swedish and New Zealand counterparts) is subject to the MP-filter; civil servants appearing before select committees are subject to the Osmo-therly Rules, which remind them that they appear on behalf of minis-ters; when Next Steps was launched, it was explicitly stated by the prime minister that ministerial responsibility was still firmly in place. The logical weakness of proclaiming the virtues of managerial auton-omy while retaining the constraint of ministerial responsibility has been manifest on occasions when operational failure has had political con-sequences which have involved ministers – as with the controversy surrounding the CSA (see Chapter 1), and the buck-passing that has accompanied high-profile breaches of prison security.

A NEW PUBLIC LAW?

Legal nostrums are not a panacea for the various problems identified in this chapter. The pathology of excessive legalism – a plethora of rules and red tape – is not an attractive prospect. But the reliance on ineffective doctrines of ministerial responsibility, the consequent underdevelopment of constitutional and administrative law, and the hostility towards legal codes and frameworks (whether one is talking about the resistance to the idea of putting Civil Service codes onto a statutory footing or Mr Waldegrave's horror at the idea of letting lawyers get anywhere near the grievance machinery of the Citizen's Charter) are regrettable and counterproductive. Later, in Chapter 8, we will discover some of the similarities between the Next Steps and the Swedish model of public administration: but we will also encounter important differences – not least the fact that the equivalents to executive agencies (autonomous boards) responsible for the delivery of public services in Sweden are subject to a tough regime of admin-istrative law, including a powerful ombudsman and public rights of access to information. In New Zealand too there is elaborate statutory regulation of the public service, direct access to an ombudsman, and freedom of information legislation.

There is of course a regime (albeit a fragmented one) of UK admin-istrative law: for instance, the jurisdiction of the PCA (and the NHS and Local Government ombudsmen) and his reports, in which he identifies 'maladministration', say a lot about what constitutes good admin-istrative practice. The common law duties to act 'fairly' (building upon the old principles of 'natural justice') and 'reasonably', enforceable through judicial review, lay down standards of good administration and respect for individuals. The system of tribunals dealing with appeals from administrative decisions and planning inquiries was mentioned in Chapter 1. But by comparison with other advanced democracies this amounts to a pretty thin system of administrative law.

There have over the years been various proposals for justiciable codes of good administrative practice. A proposal for such a code by the legal reform group JUSTICE (JUSTICE, 1971), covering matters like the right to be heard, avoidance of retrospectivity, decisions to be taken within a reasonable time, duty of public authorities to supply material information, and the requirement for reasoned decisions, was later endorsed in the unofficial JUSTICE–All Souls Review (1988). The latter report said that such a code should be drawn up with reference to the relevant Council of Europe's Committee of Ministers' Resolutions on the Protection of the Individual in relation to the Acts of Administrative Authorities, and should be supplemented by reference to the 1971 JUSTICE Report, the reports of the ombudsman, and the principles enunciated by the courts in judicial review proceedings. This proposal is endorsed by Lewis and Birkinshaw (1993), who draw interesting lessons from the United States (with its Administrative Procedure Act) and Australia (with its Administrative Review Council), and suggest that comparable developments are needed in the UK. But none of these proposals has been implemented in law.

There have, however, been a number of administrative steps which together set out an agenda for a new administrative law. The twin notions of consumer 'empowerment' through the setting of standards and provision of procedures for the redress of grievance, which underlies the Citizen's Charter, and open government, which underlies the White Paper of that name (1993) and its code, represent tentative steps in the direction of what could be a really strong system of administrative law, if the next stride could be taken – that of transforming them from exhortation into law. So far, however, there has been very little serious public debate about the development of a new public law in response to the new public management. Such a debate is long overdue. This is an issue to which we will return in our concluding chapter.

5

Public Administration, Public Management and the Law

In this chapter we shall try to provide a thumbnail sketch of the role of the law in public management and administration and explore its implications. This will provide some of the background for the case studies in Chapter 7 and comparisons with Sweden and New Zealand in Chapter 8, and for our concluding chapter.

THE ABSENCE OF A LEGAL FRAMEWORK

To a constitutionally aware visitor from Mars, or even from Sweden or New Zealand, who was taken on a tour of Whitehall, one of the most striking characteristics of the British Civil Service would be that its structure and the arrangements for accountability owe almost nothing to statute, and very little to the common law. Public management and administration in the United Kingdom are largely extra-legal, carried out in an arena that is literally invisible to the legal system and is not conceived as having legal significance unless it impinges on the liberties of individuals. There is indeed a deep-rooted suspicion among British ministers and civil servants about any suggestion that the Civil Service and central administrative arrangements should be put onto a firmer legal footing.

Central government's administrative arrangements in the United Kingdom are almost entirely made under a combination of Orders in Council promulgated under the royal prerogative (see below) and administrative fiat — decisions taken by ministers, not normally submitted to Parliament for approval, and then put into effect by organizational redisposition, lacking any legal dimensions.

THE LEGAL BASES OF CENTRAL GOVERNMENT IN THE UNITED KINGDOM

Despite the absence of a legal framework for Whitehall, there are a number of statutes which regulate the operation of the Civil Service and government departments, but they are for the most part interstitial, filling in gaps between other, non-statutory rules. So, for instance, the Ministers of the Crown Act 1975 enables functions to be transferred from one department to another, or from one minister to another, by Order in Council. But neither these Orders in Council, nor the Civil Service Order in Council (which contains most of the rules about the organization of the Civil Service), specify what departments there shall be, let alone what ministers there shall be. Those matters are hardly prescribed or even formally acknowledged by law at all, but simply recognized implicitly as realities to be acknowledged and accommodated.

Students of Cabinet and prime ministerial government – the very heart of the British Constitution – will look in vain for any substantial guidance in primary legal sources. As de Smith and Brazier observe:

> The Cabinet and the Prime Minister ... are hardly recognised in the statute book and they are almost invisible in the law reports. The Prime Minister ... was not mentioned in an Act of Parliament until 1917, and the main statutes relating to his office are those providing for his salary and pension. His powers and duties are determined almost exclusively by convention and usage. The cabinet has been virtually ostracised by the parliamentary draftsman. It appeared in 1937 (also in the context of ministerial salaries) but has made little further progress towards statutory recognition. Its composition, mode of selection, powers and procedures have to be elicited from political announcements, inference, breaches of confidence and optimistic speculation. The strict law of the constitution tells us as much and as little about political parties and the Leader of the Opposition. (de Smith and Brazier, 1994: 172–3)

It is by convention that the monarch appoints a prime minister, and by tradition that the prime minister appoints a Secretary of State (technically only one, whose office in modern times has come to be shared between a dozen or so senior departmental ministers). But once appointed, the Secretary of State has legal personality and is recognized as having the legal authority to exercise the various functions that have been granted by statute or derive from the royal prerogative and the common law (see later). The Martian would find this, surely, a remarkable case of levitation, with structures held up by nothing but convention and tradition and a few floating struts (though if there were no gravity on Mars, or if our visitor came from outer space where gravity does not exist, it might seem quite unsurprising).

Other Acts which impinge on how the Civil Service operates include:

- the Government Trading Funds Act 1973 and the Government Trading Act 1990, which enable certain functions of government, in particular those of some of the more 'commercial' Next Steps agencies, to be carried on as trading activities;
- the Deregulation and Contracting Out Act 1994, which facilitates the deregulation of private activity and, more relevantly for our purposes, the contracting out of functions hitherto performed by government departments;
- the Civil Service (Management Functions) Act 1992, which enables management functions of government departments to be transferred to civil servants such as chief executives of Next Steps agencies.

But these measures do not constitute the Civil Service, and indeed the Civil Service is nowhere defined by statute. Again, these measures are superimposed upon an almost floating organization having virtually no visible means of legal support. They serve, for the most part, to facilitate the operation and in particular the commercialization of government.

In addition to its statutory powers, the government possesses a number of extraordinary governmental powers, such as the conduct of foreign affairs and defence and the making of ministerial and other appointments. These are for the most part derived from the 'royal prerogative', defined by Blackstone as 'that special preeminence which the King hath, over and above all other persons, and out of the ordinary course of the common law, in right of his royal dignity' (1 Bl. Com.; Blackstone, 1825: 239). The power to organize and reorganize the Civil Service is one of these prerogative powers.

For our purposes, the point about all of these powers is that they are not derived from statute; they are subject only to ministerial responsibility to Parliament and the safeguards that have been developed by the courts via judicial review. Changing the terms and conditions of service of civil servants has been held to be in principle justiciable, as long as national security is not involved, so that for instance the Crown should consult the unions it has traditionally consulted before altering these employment provisions (*Council of Civil Service Unions* v *Minister for the Civil Service* [1985] AC 374, HL). But the question of whether other arrangements in the Civil Service, for instance the creation or merging of executive agencies, would be subject to judicial review has never been raised. However, since it does not affect the interests of individuals or indentifiable groups or public interests, the general assumption is that judicial review of these arrangements would not be possible (but see Freedland, 1996).

Despite the lack of a firm legal basis for management and administration in central government, we obviously do have a Civil Service that operates by and large in an orderly fashion and generally within the bounds of the law, and which does not often act in breach of the standards of propriety that are expected of the state bureaucracy in a Western democracy. This is partly attributable to the strengths of a public service culture which has developed over many years; but it also owes a good deal to the Civil Service Order in Council 1870, which gave effect to the principles set out in the Northcote Trevelyan Report of 1854 – namely recruitment on merit of a professional, permanent, non-partisan Civil Service. These are principally concerned with recruitment to the service rather than with regulating relationships between civil servants and ministers or prescribing procedures for the conduct of government, though, as we will see later, it has been decided for the first time to adopt a formal Civil Service code of conduct (see Appendix 2).

Instead of resort to detailed statutory regulation of procedures and relationships in the service (or to judicial review, which has virtually no part to play in the regulation of intra-governmental relationships), reliance is traditionally placed on the non-legal rules of the constitution, notably the doctrines of ministerial responsibility to Parliament, aided by the PCA, whose office is founded on statute, and who investigates citizens' grievances referred to him or her by MPs.

The law regards ministers and civil servants as one composite entity. Thus in *Carltona* v *Commissioner of Works* [1943] 2 All ER 560, in which a wartime requisitioning order was challenged by a factory owner on the grounds that the order had been signed by a civil servant without any reference to his ministers, the Court of Appeal accepted that, even though a minister is constitutionally responsible for departmental decisions, public business could not be carried on if ministerial powers were not in practice exercised by officials. In such a case the minister is ultimately answerable to Parliament for what is done in his or her name, and this is regarded as a sufficient safeguard of good government – an assumption that is weaker than it was during the Second World War years (but see Freedland, 1996).

Other props which maintain the Civil Service on a constitutional basis are the availability of judicial review for unlawful activity to persons outside the service who are aggrieved about decisions of government; the vigilance of the press; and that nebulous but crucially important entity, the public service ethic. These have combined to constrain what civil servants and ministers do and how they operate.

But there are signs that these constraints are no longer considered sufficient to secure what is often called 'good government', in the sense of efficient, effective and accountable government. This accounts for the appointment of Sir Richard Scott to inquire into the issues surrounding the issue of Public Interest Immunity certificates in the trials of defendants for alleged breach of the ban on exports of arms to Iraq in 1993 (Scott, 1996), the establishment of the Committee of Inquiry into Standards in Public Life under the chairmanship of Lord Nolan in 1994, and pressure from the TCSC of the House of Commons for clarification of the relationships between ministers and civil servants. Concern about these matters is reflected in modest steps, for the most part non-statutory, such as the appointments of 'complaints adjudicators' (see Chapter 3) in some agencies, the Open Government White Paper of 1993 (also noted in Chapter 3), and the acceptance by the government in 1995 of the case for a Civil Service code of conduct (see next chapter).

THE ROLE OF THE COURTS

Not only is the Westminster Parliament excluded from a role in controlling, prescribing, or even ratifying or vetoing, structural change in the United Kingdom's Civil Service, but so also is the judiciary; for it is less easy for the courts to exercise a supervisory jurisdiction over public activity that is carried on under purely administrative, non-statutory powers, and does not generally directly affect the rights or liberties of individuals, than over statutorily established and defined institutions, procedures and functions. By contrast, in the area of local government, which has a statutory basis and is subject to a strict *ultra vires* rule, the courts have always played an important role.

This is in part because in law ministers and civil servants in central government are one, so that the court cannot entertain applications for judicial review made by one part of central government against the other (though it is not uncommon for local government to bring judicial review proceedings against central departments); and partly because the courts generally claim, when judicially reviewing the administration, to be giving effect to the will of Parliament as expressed in legislation. If Parliament has not expressed its will through the enactment of a statute, the courts do not have that basis for intervening.

Another reason why it is hard for the courts to intervene in non-statutory, extra-legal administrative matters is that the limits of administrative and managerial power are less tangible when expressed in skeleton form only in an Order in Council, and otherwise left to purely administrative or managerial practice, than they would be if they were expressed in statutory form. There is commonly nothing for the courts to bite on in the institutional arrangements in the British Civil Service.

There is in any case a school of thought which is more generally sceptical of the suitability of the judicial process – in any democratic system of government – to second-guess the decisions of politicians and administrators who are ultimately, albeit imperfectly, accountable to an electorate. Moreover, litigation is an adversarial process arising out of a dispute between parties: the evidence before the court is peculiar to the matter at issue, and is a poor basis for making broader judgements about the rights and wrongs of policy and administration.

IMPLICATIONS OF THE ABSENCE OF LAW FROM PUBLIC ADMINISTRATION

Statutory bodies may do only those things that they are empowered by Parliament to do. One implication of the lack of a statutory framework for much public administration is that non-statutory bodies such as ministers, and holders of many public offices such as the Metropolitan Police Commissioner, enjoy some of the same freedom of action as individuals, so that they may do anything that is not specifically unlawful.

In *Malone* v *Metropolitan Police Commissioner* [1979] Ch. 344, for instance, the Metropolitan Police Commissioner had authorized the tapping of the telephone of Malone. The court decided that tapping was not at that time unlawful, as it did not involve trespassing on the plaintiff's land, and so the plaintiff had no remedy. If the Metropolitan Police Commissioner were a statutory office-holder, then he or she would be permitted to do only those things provided for in the statute, and it is most unlikely he or she would have been granted a general power to authorize telephone tapping without an elaborate set of safeguards. After that case, and a ruling by the European Court of Human Rights that found Britain to be in breach of Article 8 of the European Convention on Human Rights (respect for private life and correspondence), telephone tapping was put on a statutory basis. The point that we derive from the case still stands, however: non-statutory public bodies have the same freedom of action as individuals.

We noted in Chapter 1 the need for appropriate standards to be defined and followed, and for the formulation of criteria against which performance can be measured if accountability is to be imposed effectively. In the absence of formal statutory provisions for the organization and accountability of the Civil Service, relationships and procedures are regulated to a considerable degree by codes of various kinds – 'quasi-legislation' in legal terminology (Megarry, 1944; Ganz, 1987) – which

provide the criteria for accountability. These rules are generally formulated by government, in the form of written guidelines and commitments, but they are not legally enforceable.

We have already noted that relations between ministers, civil servants and Parliament are set out in *Departmental Evidence and Response to
Select Committees* (1994; commonly known as the Osmotherly Rules).
Cabinet procedures and ministerial conduct are laid down in *Questions of
Procedure for Ministers* (1992 as amended in 1994 and 1996); the
executive agencies were established in accordance with principles set
out in the White Paper *Improving Management in Government: The Next
Steps* (1988); and standards of service to be provided to individuals by
central government's agencies are set out not in statutes, but in the
Citizen's Charter and the various sectoral charters that have flowed from
it. Moreover, the duties of particular agencies to government departments are laid down in framework documents and annual performance
agreements; and in 1993 the government instituted a voluntary, non-
statutory system for the disclosure of information to individuals in its
White Paper on *Open Government* (Cm 2290).

Important points for the purposes of this discussion about the use of
quasi-legislation include the fact that it excludes Parliament from any
role in formulating or enforcing the rules, and it is often not published.
It cannot, save exceptionally, give rise to legally enforceable rights for
any of the affected parties – civil servants, ministers, or members of the
public receiving or applying for public services. On the other hand,
quasi-legislation can play an important part in determining how public
officials interpret their legal duties, it can help the PCA to deal with
grievances, drawing upon it for standards and its use does represent a
kind of 'normativization' of government which has become increasingly
influential and useful as a technique in the last decade or so.

But by no means all of the relationships between ministers, civil
servants and Parliament are regulated by written quasi-legislation.
Much is still left to tradition, practice and pragmatism. There are of
course conventions and understandings about this, but these are widely
seen to be ineffective and inadequate, as is reflected in the TCSC Report
on the Civil Service (1994) and the *First Report of the Committee on
Standards in Public Life* (the Nolan Committee) in May 1995, both of
which recommended a code for civil servants, and clarification of the
ground rules for ministers and MPs (see also Chapter 6). The government has accepted these recommendations (1995, Cm 2931).

The TCSC and, since the end of 1995, its successor, the Public
Service Committee, whose role in the parliamentary scrutiny of public
service reforms has already been mentioned, has made a substantial
contribution to the debate about the need to tighten up and consolidate
the existing codes, practices and understandings. Its contribution in the

1980s to the promulgations and revision of the Armstrong Memorandum (see Appendix 1), which set out extra-legal guidelines on the relationship between ministers and civil servants, and to the more recent introduction of a Civil Service code, is considered in the next chapter.

PUBLIC ACCESS TO INFORMATION

English law condones a high degree of secrecy within government, and the latter has not yet introduced a regime that gives much public access to such information. The absence of statutory regulation of public administration and management encourages the view that public bodies are entitled to the same or equivalent protection from scrutiny as private bodies. So, for instance, public bodies have some of the same rights to protection of confidentiality as private bodies enjoy.

Thus in *A.G.* v *Jonathan Cape* ([1976] QB 75 – the Crossman Diaries case) and *A.G.* v *Guardian Newspapers (No. 2)* ([1990] 1 AC 109 – the Spycatcher case), the courts decided that information received or communicated to a minister or a civil servant in confidence should not in principle be disclosed so long as it retains the quality of confidentiality without the consent of 'the Crown', in the same way as commercial information or communications between husbands and wives ought not to be disclosed. The duty of confidentiality arises therefore from the circumstances in which information is communicated – in confidence – regardless of public interests in information about iniquitous behaviour by public servants, for instance, being made public.

The only concession to the fact that there might be public interests in the disclosure of 'governmental' or 'official' information in some circumstances is that, where discretionary remedies such as injunctions are claimed, public interest considerations may lead to different treatment of public and private bodies. So in *A.G.* v *Jonathan Cape* the court indicated that it would not prevent unlawful disclosure of confidential information unless satisfied that it would be contrary to the public interest for it to be disclosed (in that case the information was eleven years old, and it was not considered against the public interest for it to be disclosed after so long a period).

Sunshine is a powerful disinfectant. In the United States there are 'Government in the Sunshine' Acts giving public access to government information. In many jurisdictions there are 'whistleblowers' charters' which protect public servants who disclose iniquity in government from sanctions. In the United Kingdom whistling is regarded as bad manners, and the sun does not shine very strongly on government (but see the *First Report of the Committee on Standards in Public Life*, 1995, Cm 2850: para. 3.53–3.54). The interconnected doctrines of ministerial responsibility and of Civil Service unity with the government of the day, which discourage civil servants from speaking out of turn for fear of contradicting or embarrassing their ministers, are substantially to blame for this.

There are important statutory provisions for public access to some information, for example to personal records by the subject of the information. In 1993 the White Paper on *Open Government* promised increased voluntary disclosure of information by government departments. The mechanism adopted was a code drawn up by government but not submitted to Parliament for approval or amendment, backed up with a possibility – not a right – of access to the PCA via the MP in case of refusals of disclosure. (In New Zealand and Sweden, the two countries we shall be using in Chapter 8 to make comparisons, there are statutory freedom of information regimes.) The preference for non-legal regulation via a code backed up by indirect access to the PCA is characteristic of the British distaste for law in public administration, and of the preference for political mechanisms of accountability.

REDRESS OF GRIEVANCES: THE ROLE OF THE COURTS

Outside the field of the actual organization of the Civil Service, the Crown is subject to judicial review at the instance of aggrieved individuals in many respects, just as other public bodies are, such as local authorities. Broadly, the grounds for judicial review are illegality, procedural impropriety and 'irrationality'. The grounds have been developed by the courts and are not codified or laid down by statute, save to the extent that illegality means that there has been a breach of requirements in a statute. The requirements of procedural propriety (developed from the ancient principles of 'natural justice') impose duties of fairness on decision makers, giving those affected by a decision an opportunity to put their own points of view and requiring unbiased decision making. 'Rationality' is a difficult concept, but it requires a decision maker not to take account of irrelevant considerations, to pay attention to relevant considerations, and to act in good faith.

Overall it may be said that judicial review of a decision may be available if:

- it is technically illegal;
- a power is being exercised for an improper purpose;
- an unfair procedure has been adopted;
- a discretion has been delegated or 'fettered';
- legitimate expectations have been disappointed;
- irrelevant considerations have been taken into account or relevant ones left out of account;

- a decision is so unreasonable that no reasonable minister or other official would have so decided.

But there are very tight time limits for applying for judicial review, and the remedies are generally limited to quashing decisions and requiring the decision maker to reconsider the matter as required by law (see generally Wade and Forsyth, 1994 and De Smith; Woolf and Jowell, 1995).

The Crown possesses many important statutory powers covering the raising and spending of taxation, compulsory acquisition of property for specified purposes such as road building, control of land use (with local authorities), licensing activity and so on. These powers are generally subject to procedural requirements and formality in their exercise, and there is commonly a right of appeal to an independent tribunal (the British equivalent of the Swedish 'administrative courts': see Chapter 8) or an inquiry.

For instance, if land is to be acquired compulsorily for local or central government purposes, a formal order must be served on the owner, the grounds for acquisition must be specified and must fall within a legally recognized category, and there is provision for appeal. In the latter case, an inquiry is held, the minister (or the inquiry inspector, who is a civil servant acting on the minister's behalf) decides, there may then be an appeal to the court, and compensation is fixed according to legal criteria.

If a person objects to his or her tax assessment by the Inland Revenue, an appeal lies to General or Special Commissioners of Income Tax. There are many such tribunals dealing with appeals against administrative decisions. Provisions of this kind serve to regulate the exercise of power, to protect individuals, and to require public justification to impartial officials – an inspector at a planning inquiry or the chair and members of an administrative tribunal, for instance – to be given for state action.

Overall, however, judicial review or appeals to the courts or tribunals cover only the range of grievances where a complaint is of unlawful conduct, namely technical illegality, unfair procedures, abuse of power, or unreasonableness. In practice these grounds are narrow – they do not include inefficiency, ineptness, lack of consideration, lack of funds, for instance – and judicial review is not realistically available to most individuals with grievances about government action. Remedies in such cases almost never include compensation.

In any case, many grievances about government – for instance, that taxes are too high or that crime rates are rising – are about issues of policy rather than administration. Here the only 'remedies' (if any) lie in political action, such as lobbying, demonstrating, or threatening to withhold one's vote at the next election.

THE PARLIAMENTARY COMMISSIONER FOR ADMINISTRATION: THE BRITISH OMBUDSMAN

Where a complaint is of something short of illegality, the principal recourses are to internal complaints processes and the PCA. As we saw in Chapter 3, the Citizen's Charter encourages the use of these various internal channels of complaint by spelling out standards of conduct and service and requiring complaints procedures to be put in place and drawn to the attention of the public.

The PCA was established by statute in 1967. The office is something of a hybrid, borrowing in some of its aspects from arrangements in Sweden and New Zealand which we consider in Chapter 8, but peculiarly British in many respects. Like the ombusdmen in Sweden and New Zealand, the appointment is non-political, and the holder is an officer of Parliament – the House of Commons. He or she reports to a select committee, and it is this relationship with the select committee that places agencies and departments under pressure to comply with recommendations (a good example is in the case study of the Employment Service in Chapter 7), although, as is the case with most ombudsmen, his or her recommendations are not legally enforceable. In Sweden too the ombudsman has a special relationship with a parliamentary committee (the Committee on the Constitution), and a link with Parliament in this way enhances the authority of an ombudsman.

The PCA has power to deal with complaints of maladministration, but not illegality, and in this respect he or she differs radically from the Swedish and New Zealand ombudsmen, who may consider complaints of illegality. A question for consideration would be whether the jurisdiction of the British PCA should also embrace illegality.

The PCA may only deal with complaints that have been referred to him or her by an MP, and the absence of direct access contrasts strongly with most other ombudsmen, including those in New Zealand and Sweden. The PCA has expressed a desire to see this filter removed on a number of occasions (*Annual Report*, 1993–4: para. 2), though many MPs have been reluctant to sever the link, which was designed in the first place to maintain their representative role as grievance chasers on behalf of their contituents. Unlike the ombudsmen in Sweden and New Zealand – and many others – he or she has no right to take initiatives in investigating maladministration.

Despite these limitations on his or her powers, the PCA's activities have increased in range considerably over the last few years. The PCA has indicated, as mentioned in Chapter 3, that he regards breach of the standards laid down in the Citizen's Charters as *prima facie* evidence of maladministration if those standards are sufficiently precise (*Annual Report*, 1993–4: para. 6); and he has the function of dealing with complaints of refusal of access to information under the *Open Government* White Paper (as to which see *Annual Report*, 1993–4: para. 3; *Second Report*, 1994–5, HC 91); he has begun to elaborate on the meaning of maladministration with a view to disseminating 'best practice' (*Annual Report*, 1993–4: para. 7); and he has the power to investigate 'maladministration' in the provision of 'contracted out' services (Deregulation and Contracting Out Act 1994, section 72). But the principal points of contrast with other ombudsmen are the lack of direct access and the inability to take initiatives or promulgate good practice.

THE CROWN: RELATIONS BETWEEN DEPARTMENTS, MINISTERS AND CIVIL SERVANTS

Civil servants and ministers are Crown servants – descendants of the powerful courtiers who once served absolute monarchs – and administration and management in central government are carried on in the name of the Crown. But all is not what it seems in English public law, and just as the Cabinet is not a piece of furniture, so the Crown is not just a piece of jewellery. In law the Crown is the fountain of law, justice and public policy, though these functions are heavily overlain with statute and convention. The Crown has legal personality of its own: it is a corporation, with full legal capacity, perpetual succession ('the king never dies'), and unlimited liability.

The continuation of reliance on the concept of the Crown at the core of the constitution affects not only the role of Parliament in public administration and management, but also the legal basis for much Civil Service activity, the availability of access to the courts where administrative and management arrangements may be questioned, and the normative basis of public administration and management.

The law has increasingly drawn a distinction between the apolitical Crown – the constitutional monarch of the day – and the political Crown – the institutions of central government (see *M.* v *Home Office* [1993] 3 WLR 433, in which the House of Lords upheld a contempt of court ruling against the Home Secretary for not complying with an injunction in a political asylum case). Holdsworth called it 'the distinction between the natural and politic capacity of the king' (Holdsworth, 1924: IV, 202). In relations with outsiders (those who are not ministers, departments or civil servants), the political Crown (broadly government and the Civil Service) is subject to the jurisdiction of the courts in respect of those of its actions that are in the realm of law and 'justiciable'.

In its political persona the Crown is regarded, generally, as indivisible (*Town Investments* v *Department of the Environment* [1978] AC 359, HL). This is taken to mean that, for instance, individual departments of state and executive agencies do not have separate corporate identities. So it is considered to be impossible for departments or agencies within departments to enter into legally enforceable contractual relations with one another. Hence the contractualization of public administration that we discussed earlier can only be 'quasi-contractual' and corporatization only 'quasi-corporatization' in central government.

The indivisibility of the Crown also effectively excludes the courts from judicial review of organizational arrangements in government, as opposed to matters of technical legality or procedure that affect the rights of individuals or broader public interests. An executive agency could not apply for judicial review of actions taken by its parent department (for instance, decisions about funding, the renewal of a framework document, directions given on operational matters), because it has no separate legal personality from its parent. Thus the law is virtually excluded from involvement in the executive agency arrangements, and they are the concern only of ministers and their departments, and of Parliament when exercising its functions in the scrutiny of public administration and management.

The powers of the Crown are generally, of course, exercised by ministers to whom functions have been delegated by the Crown, and in doing so ministers are politically accountable to Parliament (see Chapter 1). Under the Civil Service (Management Functions) Act 1992, some of these functions may be delegated to civil servants. In particular, section 2 provides that any statutory powers relating to the appointment and management of civil servants which require the sanction of ministers can, if the minister so desires, be exercised without such sanction, or subject to stipulated conditions.

The main effect of the 1992 Act has been to facilitate the transfer of responsibility for determining pay and conditions of service in Next Steps agencies to the chief executives of those agencies. In theory, the doctrine of ministerial responsibility remains intact, because decisions about such transfers of functions are taken by ministers, who can reverse those decisions at their discretion; but in practice, the Act – and indeed the underlying rationale of the Next Steps programme itself – entails a significant transfer of day-to-day responsibility for the administrative or operational functions of central government from ministers to senior civil servants.

Ministers are also legally liable for their own unlawful acts and those of their departments and civil servants; that is, they are subject to civil and criminal proceedings and to judicial review. Ministers acting in their official capacity are subject to the contempt jurisdiction of the courts if court orders are disobeyed (*M.* v *Home Secretary*). So the law is not excluded from supervising and controlling the exercise of powers by ministers or departments that affect individuals or broader public interests, only from supervising and controlling the organizational arrangements within government. And, significantly, Parliament too is excluded from an input into these arrangements save to the extent that – as will be shown in the next chapter – select committees like the TCSC (see above – now the Public Service Committee) carry out inquiries; usually, as has been the case with the executive agencies and the Citizen's Charter, after an initiative has been taken.

CIVIL SERVANTS AND THE PUBLIC

It is not so long ago that civil servants such as collectors and inspectors of taxes signed themselves 'Your obedient servant' when corresponding with taxpayers. It was never of course the position that civil servants were literally servants of the public: they were servants of the Crown, dismissible by the Crown at pleasure. But the point brings out the drift from the strong assumption of earlier times, even if it was not reflected in the legal position, that the Civil Service serves *the public* to the notion that it serves *the government of the day*, which has taken place almost unnoticed over the last few decades. In a sense the notion that civil servants were servants of the public was something of a mystification, since the duties were unenforceable save where a criminal offence had been committed. But they were powerful informants of parliamentary attitudes, pointing in quite a different direction from that implied in the current Osmotherly Rules and the Armstrong Memorandum (see next chapter).

The traditional view is that the Civil Service is, rightly, a permanent, professional, apolitical profession and that this status must be protected by ensuring that appointments are made on merit, by maintaining civil servants' anonymity, and by holding ministers, not civil servants, responsible to Parliament for what is done in the department (Northcote Trevelyan Report, 1854; TCSC Fifth Report 1993–4, HC 27 – I: Summary, para. 1; *The Civil Service: Taking Forward Continuity and Change*, Cm 2748, 1995: para 2.1). This view explains the dimension of 'accountability' which gives ministers the *exclusive* right to account to Parliament (Chapter 1). In relation to agencies, this conception of accountability is in sharp contrast to the position in New Zealand, for instance, where agencies are directly accountable to Parliament, and in Sweden, where they are accountable to the Parliament and the whole Cabinet, not to individual ministers (see Chapter 8).

The present position leaves open the possibility that civil servants have no independent duties to the public, the public interest or the public service ethos, but are simply there to serve and obey the government of the day. Certainly this is the main thrust of the Armstrong Memorandum – much of which is restated in the Civil Service Code (see Appendices 1 and 2). However, the latter does include paragraphs to the effect that 'civil servants should conduct themselves with integrity, impartiality and honesty' in their dealings with Ministers, Parliament and the public'. Also they 'should endeavour to deal with the affairs of the public sympathetically, efficiently, promptly and without bias or maladministration' (Cm 2748, 1995: 43–4).

Internal procedures entitle a civil servant who considers that he or she is being asked to do something improper by the minister to raise the matter with the permanent secretary in the department and ultimately with the Head of the Home Civil Service (Sir Robert Armstrong, *Note*; see HC Deb., 2 December 1987: col. 575w, and a revised version at HC (1993–4): 27 – II, p. 188 (OPSS)), but concern was widely expressed by the TCSC and many of the witnesses who took part in its inquiry that this was not a sufficient safeguard against abuse (TCSC Fifth Report, HC 27 – I, 1993–4: para. 102; *First Report of the Committee on Standards in Public Life*, 1995, Cm 2850; and see the next chapter). The right of appeal to the head of the service had apparently been used only on one occasion: this may signify the absence of a need for an appeal, or that aggrieved civil servants have little faith in the mechanism provided.

In January 1995 the government, in its White Paper issued in response to the TCSC Report, offered in a new Civil Service code (see above) an independent appeals procedure under which an aggrieved civil servant, instead of referring the matter to the Head of the Home Civil Service, would have the right to go to the Civil Service Commissioners, who would be entitled to report to Parliament if their recommendations were not acted upon (paras 2.10–2.11; see also the Nolan Report, 1995, Cm 2850, the *Government's Response*, 1995, Cm 2931 and the Civil Service Code, 1995, paras 11–13).

GOVERNMENT CONTRACTING

The fact that the Crown has legal personality means that it has the normal powers of a person to enter into contracts with third parties, to acquire and dispose of land, and so on. This is subject to its right to repudiate a contract that fetters its discretionary power as to future conduct (*The Amphitrite* [1921] 2 KB 500). Thus the contractualization of government relationships with non-governmental bodies, such as suppliers, that has been taking place in the last decade and more has been possible without the need for enabling legislation. Here, however, the courts' reluctance to interfere in contractual arrangements once made, and the peculiar position of the Crown under the *Amphitrite* rule, are causing considerable legal problems.

Generally, if there is a contract – whether between a government department and a supplier or a private purchaser and a supplier – contract law alone applies, and judicial review would not be available to seek a remedy against a government department for, for instance, illegality, unfairness or irrationality by the public party to the contract. And if there is no contract between the public body and an aggrieved party or a private body and an aggrieved party – a firm that wishes to tender for a government or private contract – the latter has no claim in private law (unless it is a case of discrimination on grounds of sex or race).

Contracting activity by the Crown is regarded by our courts in principle as essentially a private activity too, so that only private, not public law, regulates it (see *R.* v *Lord Chancellor, ex parte Hibbit and Sanders* 11 March 1993, noted by Oliver at [1993] *Public Law*, 214). This means in effect that a complaint that the Crown has acted unfairly in its decisions as to whom to contract with cannot be entertained in the courts.

But this approach on the part of the courts to contracting by the Crown is becoming increasingly untenable. European Community law regulates the public procurement process by requiring that large contracts be put out to tender. Contracting in local government (whose powers derive entirely from statute, not from common law or prerogative powers) is regarded as a public law matter, so that judicial review is available if the matter is 'justiciable' (*R.* v *Lewisham LBC, ex parte Shell UK* [1988] 1 All ER 938; *Wheeler* v *Leicester City Council* [1985] AC 1054). It is hard to see why contracting by central government should be treated differently just because contracting powers derive from statute for local government and from the common law for the Crown.

CONCLUSIONS

This discussion of public administration, public management and the law has raised a number of issues about the structure and management of the Civil Service and its relationships with government, Parliament and the public. We shall be pursuing these in subsequent chapters.

Ought the procedures for the reform of the public services to be defined and regulated by statute, thus ensuring a parliamentary input, as opposed to proceeding by Order in Council and administrative fiat in which Parliament has no role to play? Ought the relationships between civil servants, government and Parliament to be regulated by law, so as to ensure that the interests of the public in the integrity and professionalism of the service are independently protected? Should individuals with grievances against public services have more ready access to independent bodies that can investigate and seek redress? Should there be wider, legally backed access to information about government? Should the criteria against which government or those responsible for public services are to be judged be more closely defined in the many areas in which criteria can be elaborated?

In other words, should politics, public administration and management be increasingly normativized? And if so, to what extent should the normativization take a legal form, in the sense of opening up access to the courts if the norms are broken?

6

Parliament and the Reformed Civil Service

In the United Kingdom, the absence of statutory regulation of public administration and management in central government serves to reinforce a strong assumption on the parts of the courts, Parliament, ministers and civil servants that political mechanisms of accountability – in particular, ministerial accountability to Parliament, and Civil Service accountability to ministers – are appropriate and effective as checks on the abuse of power or ineffectiveness or inefficiency in the public service. This is reflected in the limitations on provisions for direct Civil Service accountability to Parliament (see Chapter 1).

PARLIAMENT AND THE REDRESS OF GRIEVANCES

It is supposed to be a fundamental principle of the British Constitution that redress of grievance comes before supply – Parliament will not grant the government the taxes it needs until its grievances and those of individuals have been redressed. This tradition used to be reflected in the Opposition's right to a number of 'Supply Days' when it could choose the subject for debate before granting supply, i.e. giving formal approval to the government's estimates of expenditure for the forthcoming tax year. These days have now been renamed 'Opposition Days' and the tradition of seeking redress of grievance before supply has almost disappeared.

The enduring affection for ministerial responsibility and the grievance-chasing role of the constituency MP, rather than administrative law, as the basis for redress of citizens' grievances against the state is reflected in the arrangements for the PCA, who may receive complaints of maladministration only if they are directed through an MP (see Chapter 5). British MPs expend considerable energies on dealing with the grievances of their constituents, and it has to be asked whether this is appropriate, given the needs of Parliament in the legislative process and the scrutiny of government policy, when redress of grievance is something that could be dealt with by ombudsmen.

The position in Britain contrasts sharply with approaches in other European countries: as Fred Ridley has observed, 'the idea of "political" rather than "legal" protection of citizens against administration is deeply embedded in British political traditions and has imprinted itself on British ways of thought' (Ridley, 1984: 4). The British approach to redress (compounded by A.V. Dicey's prejudice against the development of a separate *droit administratif*) has inhibited the development of a vigorous system of administrative law. Alternatives are being introduced – the use of internal complaints procedures is encouraged by the Citizen's Charter, and complaints adjudicators are being appointed (see Chapter 3) – but, as with many other aspects of the reform process, these developments are taking place on a non-legal, non-statutory basis.

CIVIL SERVICE ACCOUNTABILITY TO PARLIAMENT

We noted in our first chapter the doctrine that civil servants are in principle accountable to ministers and not to Parliament, although this position is being modified as agency chief executives are appointed as accounting officers, and they and other senior civil servants are called before select committees and may be subjected to intensive questioning in such matters as their responses to PCA reports (see the Employment Service case study in Chapter 7 for an example). Select committees have in recent years, particularly since the establishment of a new system of departmentally related committees in 1979 (see below), taken a substantial proportion of their evidence from civil servants.

As we also noted in Chapter 1, written answers to parliamentary questions about operational matters relating to agencies are printed in Hansard under the names of chief executives, though the constitutional niceties are preserved by retaining the name of the minister as the person to whom the question has formally been addressed.

But although these and other developments have introduced a measure of direct Civil Service accountability and given MPs an opportunity to engage in public dialogue with civil servants (sometimes in front of TV cameras, when committee hearings are televised), and allowed some light to penetrate the traditionally secret places of Whitehall, the Osmotherly Rules (see Chapter 1) give Civil Service witnesses appearing before select committees a clear reminder that ultimate responsibility remains with the minister: 'officials who give evidence to Select Committees do so on behalf of their Ministers and under their directions' (*Departmental Evidence and Response to Select Committees*, 1994: para. 38).

The government recognizes that it is open to a select committee of the House of Commons, if the minister is unwilling to agree, to summon a named civil servant to appear before them. But 'the official would remain subject to Ministerial instruction on how to answer questions and on what information to disclose. Such impasse is, however, unprecedented' (*Departmental Evidence*, 1994: para. 41). This is one manifestation of the doctrine of unity, discussed in the last chapter and restated in the Armstrong Memorandum (below: see also Appendix 1).

PARLIAMENT AND INSTITUTIONAL ARRANGEMENTS

The absence of a statutory basis or framework for the Civil Service means, as we saw in earlier chapters, that Parliament is excluded from the function that the legislature performs in most other aspects of government, and in comparable other jurisdictions: that of establishing the Civil Service, and scrutinizing and then ratifying arrangements, especially institutional arrangements, for the carrying on of public management and administration. For example, in New Zealand (as we shall see in Chapter 8), by contrast with the United Kingdom, the executive agency initiative was introduced by legislation (the State Sector Act 1988) and thus made subject at the outset to Parliamentary scrutiny and legitimation. And in Sweden too the Civil Service is subject to statutory regulation and Parliamentary scrutiny.

But although the Westminster Parliament plays a very limited legislative role in the process of administrative reform in central government, it has exercised such a role in relation to other parts of the public sector – local government, the NHS and the privatization of nationalized industries and public utilities – where the bodies concerned are established by and derive their powers from statute.

PARLIAMENT, MINISTERS AND CIVIL SERVANTS

It would not be quite accurate to suggest that Parliament exercises no monitoring functions in the context of Civil Service reform. The House of Commons select committee system, which was substantially reorganized on departmentally related lines in 1979, has played an increasingly important role in the scrutiny of the operation of executive agencies. In particular, the TCSC (now the Public Service Committee) has taken a close interest from the outset in the Next Steps initiative, and has produced a series of compendious and authoritative reports on the agencies, accompanied by a large quantity of oral and written evidence from ministers and officials as well as from experts from outside government (for references see Giddings, 1995: bibliography). And some of the other departmentally related committees have, from time to time, made a point of looking at the agencies associated with their departments (Natzler and Silk, 1995).

But select committees, however conscientious they may be, can only report and recommend; it is the government which takes the initiative in matters of reform, and which normally commands a majority on the floor of the House. Moreover, the select committees' limited resources and wide terms of reference restrict their capacity to look regularly and in depth at any one aspect.

THE TCSC AND THE ARMSTRONG MEMORANDUM

Growing tensions in the traditional relationship between senior civil servants and ministers came in for a lot of discussion in the pre-Next Steps years, particularly in the context of the Westland and Ponting affairs in the mid-1980s (we have already discussed some aspects of the Westland affair in Chapter 1). There was an inquiry into the subject by the TCSC (TCSC, 1986); and the Commons Defence Committee produced a report on the Westland case which was highly critical of the government's handling of criticisms of civil servants involved in the leaking of a document written in confidence by the Solicitor General (Defence Committee, 1986).

In response to these episodes, the then Head of the Civil Service, Sir Robert Armstrong, issued a note of guidance on 'The Duties and Responsibilities of Civil Servants in Relation to Ministers'; the version issued in February 1985 was reissued in December 1987 (Armstrong Memorandum, 1987 HC Deb., vol. 123, cols 572–5) in a modified and expanded version, taking on board observations by the two select committees and by the Council of Civil Service Unions (CCSU). Its provisions (in slightly abridged form) are set out at the end of this book, in Appendix 1.

Although, according to constitutional conventions restated in the Armstrong Memorandum, the Civil Service owes undivided allegience to the government of the day, many civil servants have been unhappy about the one-sidedness of this. Do not ministers owe a reciprocal duty towards their civil servants? The revised edition of the *Questions of Procedure for Ministers* (the code that has been developed over the years to regulate the conduct of ministers, first published by the Cabinet Office in 1992), responding to critical comments by the TCSC, noted some of the obligations owed by ministers to civil servants, including:

a duty to give fair consideration and due weight to informed
and impartial advice from civil servants, as well as to other
considerations and advice, in reaching policy decisions; the duty

to refrain from asking or instructing civil servants to do things which they should not do; a duty to ensure that influence over appointments is not abused for partisan purposes; and a duty to observe the obligations of a good employer with regard to terms and conditions of those who serve them. (para. 55)

THE CIVIL SERVICE CODE: THE 1993–4 TCSC INQUIRY

Not long after the 1992 general election, the TCSC (which, as we have already noted, had been taking a close interest in the Next Steps reforms) embarked upon a wide-ranging inquiry into the role of the Civil Service. Having taken oral evidence from an array of ministers and top officials, it published an Interim Report in July 1993. The Report (TCSC, 1993: I, para. 4) identified at least five separate elements of current concern about the Civil Service:

(i) Concern about whether the management changes in the Civil Service in recent years, most notably the Next Steps initiative, have had fundamental implications which were not anticipated at the time the reforms were initiated;

(ii) Concern about the impact on the Civil Service of the market testing initiative and the possible privatisation of some Civil Service functions (see *Competing for Quality*, 1991; TCSC, 1993, vol. I, para. 11; vol. II, pp. 105–9);

(iii) Concern about whether the formation of a higher Civil Service is suitable both for its management tasks and for the provision of good policy advice to ministers;

(iv) Concern about an alleged deterioration in standards of conduct in the Civil Service;

(v) Concern about the implications for the Civil Service of a fourth successive election victory by the same political party.

An ex-prime minister (who had first entered public life as a tax officer), Lord Callaghan, told the committee that he was 'more worried about the Civil Service than I have ever been in the 60-odd years from when I first joined it and have been associated with it' (TCSC, 1993: II, Q. 587).

In March 1993, the Chairman of the Committee asked Sir Robin Butler, Head of the Home Civil Service, 'What, in your view, are the essential values and ethics of the British Civil Service?'. To which Sir Robin replied:

impartiality, integrity and objectivity are the three which I would pick out, plus, as far as the Service is managed, selection and promotion on merit. Those, I think, are the essential characteristics, plus accountability through ministers to Parliament. I think everything flows from those five. (TCSC, 1993: II, Q. 101)

No other witnesses ventured to contradict Sir Robin's statement – perhaps because it went no further than a bland restatement of constitutional orthodoxy, and the government later restated the Butler formula in its White Paper on the Civil Service, *Continuity and Change* (White Paper, 1994: para. 2.7).

However, the FDA, the trade union representing the higher civil servants, many of whom work closely with ministers, took the opportunity to restate its long-standing dissatisfaction with the Armstrong Memorandum and to renew its earlier calls for publication of a code of ethics. Its written evidence (TCSC, 1993: II, 39) suggested that:

such a Code, including as it does the provision for a civil servant to approach an independent ombudsman, or Privy Councillors, would in our view clearly establish the relationships between civil servants and Ministers. The higher public profile of officials has aroused increasing concern about the ethical dilemmas facing civil servants. In restating the traditional convention of Ministerial responsibility, the Armstrong Code ... has been widely criticised for failing to answer questions of what a civil servant should do if he or she believes that his or her Minister is seeking to evade Ministerial responsibility by, for example, misleading the House of Commons, or if he or she is being required to do work which is properly for party political staff.

The FDA went on to note particular uncertainties in relation to:

- the role of ministers' special advisers, who are temporary civil servants, hand-picked by ministers;
- the constraints that face civil servants when giving evidence to select committees, an area where in recent years the traditionally anonymous civil servant has had to become accustomed to very public appearances, often in the full glare of media coverage, and sometimes before television cameras;
- the ambiguous lines of accountability for Next Steps agency chief executives, who are, for instance, not allowed to explain to Parliament that administrative failures are due to ministers having denied them the resources they need to perform their functions effectively.

It noted some of the issues relating to the duties of civil servants that had been raised by the Matrix Churchill affair – the subject of the Scott inquiry (Scott, 1996). And it endorsed the call by others (notably Lord

Callaghan) for a commission to examine the relationship between civil servants and ministers.

Some of these issues acquired sharp topicality from the Scott inquiry (Scott, 1996); also from William Waldegrave's observation to the TCSC (in March 1994) that there are exceptions to the duty of ministers always to tell the truth to Parliament. The latter incident moved the General Secretary of the FDA to write to *The Times* (11 March 1994) that:

> What is so remarkable about the furore that has followed [Waldegrave's statement] is the conflict of evidence about what constitutes proper behaviour for a minister in his or her dealings with Parliament ... No doubt, the absence of a written constitution, or indeed any clear and unequivocal rules ... compounds the difficulty. There should be guidelines for civil servants and government ministers in their dealings with each other, and, as importantly, with Parliament and the public. A number of civil servants feel that the incidents of ministers misleading Parliament are cause for anxiety. Their duty is that as civil servants their primary duty is to maintain confidentiality and loyal service 'for all practical purposes' to the Government of the day. Such a sweeping statement of their duties is not a tenable position, and now needs urgent review.

Meanwhile, the TCSC received a lot of evidence concerning the proposal for a code, and on the further issue of whether there should be a Civil Service statute. Sir Robin Butler submitted a memorandum (TCSC, 1993: II, 36–7) listing the 'central documents covering the conduct of civil servants'. This comprised twelve items, ranging widely in scope and status: from the Civil Service Management Code (which incorporates the Armstrong Memorandum and the rules concerning business appointments for those leaving the Civil Service), the Osmotherly Rules (on giving evidence to select committees), and *Questions of Procedure for Ministers* to codes of practice on equal opportunities for women and ethnic minorities and on the employment of people with disabilities.

Sir Robin conceded in evidence that it might be desirable to tidy up and consolidate these disparate codes, but he was opposed to a Civil Service Act on the grounds that it might introduce 'a certain inflexibility into the system'. The FDA's oral evidence endorsed the Butler point about inflexibility, but indicated that the FDA did not have a clear view about whether the code that it favoured should be incorporated in a statute. Nearly all the other evidence received by the committee in the first phase of its inquiry was hostile to the idea of legislation.

In its final report (TCSC, 1994: I, section IV), the TCSC noted evidence from some witnesses to the effect, *inter alia*, that the introduction of business-orientated values into the Civil Service might carry the risk of corruption; and that in a less homogeneous Civil Service it would be harder to preserve and transmit public service values. Predictably, official witnesses did not share this view, and the committee itself agreed that the Next Steps reforms were in principle compatible with the maintenance of the traditional values of the Civil Service. However, it warned that:

> the devolution of authority within the Civil Service and the
> disappearance of the traditional structures of control reinforces
> the need for greater vigilance about standards throughout the
> Civil Service. The disappearance of many tangible common
> features of careers in different parts of the Civil Service
> reinforces the importance of the less tangible shared values, and
> emphasises the need to make those shared characteristics better
> known and understood throughout the service. (TCSC, 1994: I,
> para. 84)

The committee went on to review (TCSC, 1994: I, section V) the existing array of Civil Service codes (including the Armstrong Memorandum), and concluded that their diversity – designed for different purposes and addressed to different audiences – made them a poor substitute for a proper code of standards: 'None communicates a clear and simple message to all civil servants and to the wider public about the standards to be upheld' (para. 101). The committee also expressed doubts about the existing mechanisms for upholding the values stated in these codes, which are based mainly on upward referral of complaints and concerns within the government machine itself:

> we believe that the existing procedures do not command the
> confidence of all civil servants. The preservation of the principles
> and values of the Civil Service is too important to be left to
> Ministers and civil servants alone. (TCSC, 1994: I, para. 102)

The committee recommended that there should be a new Civil Service code (not, it should be noted, a code of ethics), to cover the staff of all departments and agencies. Thought should also be given to extending it to quangos, particularly where they have taken over work from departments. A draft code was appended to the Report. It also rejected government arguments that an independent appeals procedure for civil servants concerned about matters of propriety and ethics would disrupt the relationship between officials and their ministers, and proposed that, in cases that cannot be resolved by internal appeal procedures, a final appeal should lie to an independent and strengthened body of the Civil Service Commissioners.

Despite its long-standing reservations on these matters, the government accepted in principle both recommendations (White Paper, 1995, Cm 2748). The committee's draft Code of Practice, with significant drafting amendments, was accepted as the basis of the new code. However, the government was undecided about the status of the code:

> It is possible for the Government to consult on and introduce a
> new Civil Service Code without legislation, by Prerogative
> action and Order in Council ... Nevertheless, the Government
> retains an open mind about the case, advanced by the Select
> Committee and others, for giving statutory backing to the rules
> in connection with the terms and conditions of employment of
> civil servants, including the new Code. It acknowledges the
> view that additional authority would be conferred on the
> proposed Civil Service Code ... by a statutory approach, and
> that such legislation, if based on cross-party consensus, could be
> an effective means of expressing and entrenching general
> agreement on the non-political nature of the Civil Service, and
> it recognises that the Select Committee recommended narrowly-
> based legislation on these lines on the basis that it could
> command wide support.' (*ibid*.: paras 2.15–2.16)

The concession that a code would be an improvement was an implicit acknowledgement that the absence of statutory regulations and provision, and reliance instead on political pressures, cannot necessarily be depended upon to secure proper conduct and public confidence in these arrangements.

The *First Report of the Committee on Standards in Public Life* (the Nolan Committee, 1995), established in response to concern about the conduct of ministers, civil servants and MPs, and about systems for the making of appointments to some public bodies, recommended that the new Civil Service Code be introduced with immediate effect, without waiting for legislation. The government accepted this and published a new draft code which would be implemented, subject to allowing time for consultation with Civil Service unions on the terms of the code, as soon as possible (*Response* 1995, Cm 2931). They also accepted in principle the Nolan Committee recommendation that the Cabinet Office should continue to survey and disseminate best practice on maintaining standards of conduct, to ensure that basic principles of conduct are being properly observed. In late 1995 a Civil Service code was at last agreed to by the government and introduced (HL Deb.; 30 October 1995, cols 146–8).

Clearly, in a period of rapid reform, problems are arising from the absence of clearly defined relationships and standards of conduct in the Civil Service, and indeed in government generally. Whether such relationships and standards of conduct should be of legal effect or contained only in quasi-legislation is of course highly politically sensitive. It is arguable, moreover, that so long as it remains an over-riding principle that civil servants – even the chief executives of Next Steps agencies, with their ostensible day-to-day autonomy in respect of 'operational' matters – must, when the chips are down, do what ministers tell them, a non-statutory code is of little more than cosmetic significance. As Massey observes:

> Without statutory backing a code of ethics is simply a symbolic adornment. In any profession where there is a lack of private practice opportunities and there is no defining statute, a code of ethics is of little value. It may serve an educative function for direct entrants from the private sector, but the situation is such that breaking the code in order to carry out a lawful ministerial instruction carries no penalty. Whilst maintaining the provisions of the code and defying the minister carries more painful consequences for the individual. (Massey, 1995: 26)

The effectiveness of a code is substantially a function of how it is policed and enforced, and the enhanced role of the Civil Service Commissioners does not look a particularly convincing answer. A statutory code (ultimately justiciable by the courts) would be another matter. Giving the task of policing observance of the code to the Parliamentary Commissioner (as proposed by the FDA) might be even better, particularly as it would enhance Parliament's role in scrutinizing public administration.

But the code is a step in the right direction. There are strong pressures to normativize political, managerial and administrative processes, and even non-statutory, extra-legal normativization through the use of quasi-legislation can serve to enhance responsibility and accountability.

PARLIAMENT AND AUDIT

Let us start this section with an anecdote: a bus driver had a number of performance targets to meet, mostly to do with the punctuality of his service. He drove past a queue of hopeful passengers without stopping, despite the fact that his bus was nearly empty. When asked by his supervisor, who had received complaints from the frustrated passengers, why he had not stopped, he explained that he would be late arriving at the terminus if he always stopped for passengers.

The role of audit, both in its traditional sense of ensuring that public money has been spent legally and in its more modern emphasis (as stated in the National Audit Act 1983) on 'efficiency, effectiveness and economy', has become increasingly important against the backcloth of the New Public Management Revolution – and it has extended beyond the traditional parliamentary framework. Audit has also become important in local government, with the Audit Commission having responsibility for audit of local government and the NHS. Its advantages over judicial review were illustrated by the reports of the District Auditor on Westminster City Council in 1994 and 1995 (Magill, 1994, 1996). As the Westminster example shows, the procedure of audit enables a much more thorough investigation of the facts to be made than could judicial review, with its adversarial procedure and its problems over discovery and access to documents.

Audit has always been a key parliamentary function. It dates back to the establishment of the PAC of the House of Commons at the instigation of Gladstone in 1861, and to the passing five years later of the Act establishing an Exchequer and Audit Department (the forerunner of the National Audit Office), headed by the Comptroller and Auditor General.

With the National Audit Act 1983, the audit of public expenditure for economy and efficiency became the function of the Comptroller and Auditor General (who became an officer of the House of Commons) and the National Audit Office (NAO). They report to the PAC. 'Value for money' audit is an important part of the NAO agenda, alongside traditional verification of financial legality and regularity. Thus the functions of the newly constituted office gained independence from the Treasury, although the Treasury still has very important functions in imposing internal control on these matters (McEldowney, 1994a).

The NAO (and the PAC, following up its reports) has focused on various areas of the Next Steps programme, including a number of value for money (VFM) reports on agencies. The first in the series, in 1989, was an account of the arrangements made by five departments to identify candidates for agency status, the setting up of these agencies, and the work of the Next Steps project team in the Cabinet Office (Baines, 1995: 101–2).

A subsequent, path-breaking report on the Department of Transport's Vehicle Inspectorate included some critical discussion of performance indicators and of quality of service, and generated some sharp exchanges with the Treasury over what were seen to be implicit criticisms of the rationale and value of establishing agencies (*ibid.*: 103–11). The Next Steps programme is, of course, an important element of government policy, and the traditional view is that audit should steer well clear of policy matters, though this is often very difficult in VFM contexts. We will look in much more detail at this NAO/PAC exercise in the context of our case study of the Vehicle Inspectorate Agency in the next chapter.

An academic case study of another VFM report (on *Creating and Safeguarding Jobs in Wales*, NAO, 1991) was critical of some apsects of the NAO's work. It concluded, however, that such studies are 'of considerable parliamentary and democratic significance' in that they greatly strengthen the ability of MPs 'to deal with the executive on the latter's own ground – that of technical expertise, economic analysis and programme evaluation' (Roberts and Pollitt, 1994: 546).

The process of normativization of public service referred to in the previous chapter is often designed to be checked by audit. Performance targets are set and then performance is audited to see whether they were met, if not why, and sometimes to impose penalties for failure to meet targets or rewards for doing so.

As illustrated by the example of the bus driver, and by the Employment Service case study account of the clashes between the PCA and the Chief Executive of that agency (Chapter 7), there are clearly lessons to be learnt about formulating targets so as to be sure that the public service's values, aims and objectives – even its ethos – are not undermined. Where targets are backed up by performance-related pay arrangements, there may even be risk of distorting what would be normal Civil Service activity. In Chapter 8 we will see that Sweden has long had in place institutional arrangements for 'auditing' public services and promoting good practice. A question for consideration is whether and how arrangements in Britain can incorporate this function.

Power (1994) has identified two models of control and accountability, Styles A and B. Audit generally conforms to Style A. The dichotomies he poses for these two styles are, respectively, between quantitative and qualitative audit, the use of a single measure or multiple measures, audit by external agency or internal agency, long-distance methods or local methods, low trust or high trust, discipline or autonomy, *ex post* control or real-time control, and the use of private experts or public dialogue. Power suggests that the benefits gained from using Style A (audit) are likely to be most visible when used in conjunction with, rather than in opposition to, Style B. Here is a strong reminder of the limitations of audit and the need to have in place other accountability mechanisms that will be concerned to promote the Style-B values.

CONCLUSIONS

For reasons already explained, Parliament has not played a significant part in instigating, or even authorizing by exercising its legislative functions, the Civil Service reform aspects of the New Public Management Revolution. But its reformed select committee system, and extended roles for its ombudsman (e.g. in monitoring the open government code) and its auditor (particularly in the context of VFM studies), have enabled it to undertake some sporadic monitoring of the impact of the changes that have taken place – sometimes (as with the work of the TCSC and the new Civil Service Code) with noticeable effect. In 1996 the newly established Public Service Committee embarked upon a major inquiry into Ministerial Accountability and Responsibility.

But the most important single reform – the Next Steps programme – has been expressly designed to dilute ministerial responsibility for the operational aspects of public administration, and hence parliamentary accountability in respect of such matters. There have been compensatory procedural changes (for instance, the answering of parliamentary questions by chief executives), and the publication of the framework agreements and performance figures of agencies have much potential for improving accountability. But the general thrust of reform has been to distance public service management from political control, removing some services and institutions from the public sector altogether, and that can only be to the detriment of parliamentary accountability. It raises important questions about the alternative mechanisms of accountability, through, for instance, improved redress of grievance procedures, open government and the role of judicial review. The comparative studies in Chapter 8 indicate the sorts of alternative that are available in systems that do not place the reliance that we do on accountability of public services to Parliament.

7

Executive Agencies and the Citizen's Charter: Three Case Studies

In our case studies of three executive agencies in this chapter, we seek to give a flavour of how the arrangements work in practice, and to assess their on-the-ground significance and, in the case of the Employment Service, how the Citizen's Charter and complaints procedures operate alongside the agency arrangements. We focus particularly on issues of accountability and efficiency. We have chosen three very different agencies in order to obtain a broad view of the workings of the initiative. Each illustrates a combination of general points and particular dimensions of the arrangements.

The first case study (about the first executive agency, the Vehicle Inspectorate) illustrates how agency arrangements have evolved from earlier reforms, how trading-fund status operates in relation to an agency, how relations with the parent department have developed under these arrangements, and in particular the role of the Advisory Group in these relationships.

The second case study looks at HMSO, a trading fund much of whose activity is closely analogous to private sector operations. It is an agency that has undergone a market testing programme and three reviews since 1988. The government decided to privatize it in 1996 subject to retaining a residual body with the title 'HMSO' in public ownership.

In the third case study (of the Employment Service), we focus on the significance of the framework document and other agency documents in the relationships between the chief executive and the parent department, the financial provisions, and arrangements for accountability to Parliament and members of the public who have dealings with the agency.

THE VEHICLE INSPECTORATE

The Vehicle Inspectorate (VI) was founded in 1964 as a division of the Ministry of Transport. The VI's main functions are to conduct all statutory annual roadworthiness tests on heavy goods vehicles and public service vehicles, to supervise the operation of the MOT scheme (the annual testing of private cars over three years of age) and enforce its standards, and to monitor drivers' hours regulations, operators' maintenance agreements and the roadworthiness of vehicles through roadside and other tests – enforcement work. It spends around £50 million per annum, of which over 60 per cent is on staff costs.

The VI's 'customers' are both vehicle owners and the department, which 'purchases' services from it. The government as a whole, for the public, also 'purchases' rather intangible and undefined benefits from the agency in the form of better road safety and environmental improvements that should flow from better vehicle conditions and control of overloading.

The background to the establishment of the VI as an agency is that consideration was given in the early 1980s to the possibility of privatizing the vehicle testing aspects of its operations. That option was rejected and the VI was reviewed in 1983, with a view to obtaining the benefits that might have resulted from privatization and in order to introduce best practice. Ron Oliver, Chief Executive of the agency at the time of writing, was appointed Project Manager in 1984. From 1985 to 1988 the recommendations of the 1983 review were implemented, and it became clear that there was a lacuna in accountability and focus in the operations of the inspectorate. Suitable models were looked for, and consideration was given to establishing a trading fund, of which there were only three in existence at that time. That option turned out not to be legally possible under the Government Trading Funds Act 1973 because the VI was not trading and was a statutory monopoly. Consideration was given to establishing the VI as a quango of some kind, but this option too was rejected because it was realized that the accountability arrangements could not be satisfactory.

At about this time the Next Steps report was produced and the VI was chosen as one of twelve candidates for testing the model. The VI Framework Document was the first to be drafted under the Next Steps initiative, and the VI became the first agency. The arrangements embody many of the proposals that had been made in the 1983 review of the VI.

The Project Director became Chief Executive when the agency was established, for a fixed period. The post was readvertised in 1994 and the existing Chief Executive was reappointed. He regards the executive agency arrangements as forming part of a package, linked to the trading-fund status, that have increased his accountability to the public and to Parliament. It has focused relationships, and had an immense psychological effect in the agency, to the extent that it is now in his view a very different organization.

On the other hand there can be tension between the Chief Executive and the central department over their respective responsibilities, particularly where these are unclear. For instance, the Chief Executive formally gained responsibility from 1 April 1994 for the pay and grading of staff. But some other personnel matters, such as security, remained the responsibility of the department. And it seems likely that, while the arrangements on pay and grading are formally delegated, the department and the Treasury will retain considerable control.

Relationships with the Department

In the department, the agency has two sets of contacts. The Executive Agencies Division acts as the 'banker and shareholder' looking at overall financial and quality performance, while the Road and Vehicle Safety Directorate is the 'customer' for most of the services directly paid for by government. These interests are formally brought together in the agency's Advisory Board.

Discussion has been taking place about the relationship between the Chief Executive and the Secretary of State, and who is responsible for what. The position of the department is that the Secretary of State is accountable for the VI in the sense of being obliged to give an account to Parliament, except for operational matters, and the Chief Executive is responsible for implementing the framework document and agreements with the department. Here there is a difficult grey area in ministerial accountability which has not as yet been resolved in the VI. In the aftermath of accountability and responsibility problems in, for instance, the Prison Service and the CSA (see Chapter 1), the Secretary of State is giving more attention to matters of accountability for the VI and where responsibility – in whatever sense that term is used – lies, and this is resulting in increasing contact between the Secretary of State and the agency.

The Advisory Board

In these relationships, the Advisory Board to the VI has an interesting and developing role. The Advisory Board was set up by the department in 1986, and theoretically acts as a channel of communication between the Secretary of State on one hand, and two sister interests, the VI and its departmental customers, on the other.

There are two separate customers in the department: the 'purchasers' of enforcement services provided by the agency, and 'policy customers'.

The Advisory Board has acted as mediator in conflicts between the departmental customers and the agency: for instance, in 1991 some 20 per cent of light goods vehicle testing work was transferred to MOT garages, so that the VI lost a large part of its business. There were conflicts between the department's policy objectives and its 'purchasing' arm on this decision to transfer work from the VI. The Advisory Board was able to bring these interests together, and reached a compromise under which the VI was to be permitted to compete for the light goods vehicle work. It succeeded in obtaining some of this work, and the experience of having to compete had a significant effect on staff attitudes. But on occasions the Secretary of State has dealt directly with the VI and with the departmental customers, to ask for advice directly from the VI on policy matters, and so bypass the Advisory Board.

Financial and Auditing Arrangments

In April 1991 the VI became the first agency to be awarded trading-fund status under the Government Trading Act 1990, which overcame the difficulties which had prevented the VI obtaining that status earlier. The agency and its Chief Executive have stewardship of its assets (which are formally owned by the Department of Transport) and has to account for them. Under the Government Trading Act, the Chief Executive is appointed by the Treasury, not by the permanent secretary in the department, to be Head of the Trading Fund, and he is a full accounting officer, not simply an agency accounting officer. He is personally responsible for signing the fund's financial statement, presents the accounts directly to Parliament, and accounts directly to Parliament in financial matters. Thus he has considerable independence from the department and direct accountability to Parliament as a result of the trading fund.

The financial objectives of the fund are laid upon the Minister under the Government Trading Funds Act 1973, and are as follows:

i.   managing the funded operations so that the revenue of the fund is not less than sufficient taking one year with another to meet outgoings that are properly chargeable to revenue account; and

ii. achieving such further financial objectives as the Treasury may from time to time, by minute laid before the House of Commons, indicate as having been determined by the Minister, with Treasury concurrence, to be desirable of achievement.

Thus the fund has to manage its affairs within the income it generates, although it does have the power within limits to raise loans from the parent department, Transport. It is supposed to achieve a real return on capital employed in the form of an operating surplus expressed as a percentage of net assets. This was set at 6 per cent for 1993–4; 11.3 per cent was achieved. This has been attributed to improved operational efficiency and a lower asset base resulting from the declining property values (*Next Steps Review*, 1994).

The VI was the first executive agency to be the subject of an NAO VFM study (see Chapter 6) and Report by the Comptroller and Auditor General (1992), followed up by a PAC Report (Nineteenth Report, HC 118, 1992–3) and a Treasury Minute (Cm 2175, 1993).

The NAO Report was broadly supportive of the VI and found that there had been substantial improvements in its performance since it acquired agency status. The main concerns were whether the improvements could be attributed to agency status, or whether they could have taken place without the additional delegated powers that status had brought. The conclusion on this point was that the changes might not have taken place at all and would not have proceeded at the same pace if the inspectorate had not been an agency, because the agency status provided the opportunity and was used as a catalyst to change attitudes in the VI. This was the case put strongly to them by the Chief Executive.

Having completed its VFM survey, the NAO felt that other agencies could benefit from the positive experience of the VI in a number of fields: creating a corporate identity, encouraging teamwork, clarifying their relationship with their 'customers' both in the department and among the public, introducing customer service initiatives, delegating functions, improving communication within the agency, involving staff in decision making, and improving efficiency by working to meet clear and taut targets.

However, the NAO Report expressed concern that after three years as an agency, during which substantial efficiency savings had been made, the VI had found it increasingly difficult to make the savings required to meet their targets. (For 1993–4, after the NAO Report, these were set at 5 per cent, and 5.6 per cent was achieved.) It was questionable whether more large improvements could be made without further developments of the agency arrangements, especially relating to their use of underutilized assets and the question of whether they could seek new 'business'. There was also a question whether additional freedoms should be delegated to the Chief Executive by the department and the Treasury, including greater flexibility in staffing and increased financial delegations: 'the policy parameters within which the Inspectorate operate have an important impact on the scope for further improvements in efficiency' (*ibid.*: para. 15). These were matters for the Treasury and the department, and the point, and indeed the whole report, illustrates how it is not only the agency but also the department and Treasury whose accountability may be sharpened by agency status.

Other difficulties on which the NAO focused related to the need to develop measures to give a better indication of the VI's overall contribution to the department's achievement of road safety and environmental targets; the absence of interest in outputs in terms of the impact of their activities on road safety and the environment, rather than inputs; the need for more detailed costing and research before introducing additional customer service initiatives; and possibly further delegation to district officers using 'mini-framework documents'. But the report concluded that, even with such practical improvements, without policy changes the scope for radical improvements would become exhausted and management might find further gains more difficult. Again, responsibility for this would rest with the department rather than with the agency.

Relationships with Parliament

The NAO Report was agreed to by the department and the agency, and the PAC decided to take evidence from the inspectorate and the department on the progress that the VI had made. Its inquiry and report were more critical in tone than the NAO Report. The PAC felt that there were significant weaknesses in the design of the index that the VI had produced to show that its efficiency had increased: some matters gave a misleading impression. The PAC picked up on the fact that only 30 per cent of the VI staff felt that it was characterized by efficient working practices, and they recommended that staff should be involved in securing practical improvements in efficiency.

A relatively large proportion of vehicle operators were unaware of the customer services that were available, and two of the initiatives taken by the inspectorate – Saturday opening and voluntary testing of brakes – were believed to be unsuccessful by some 60 per cent of the staff. Although more enforcement work was being carried out, nearly a quarter of staff thought that the standard of enforcement activity had deteriorated, and the PAC recommended that hard evidence of the current quality of this work should be obtained.

The PAC was in many respects critical of the department in its relations with the VI. The department had not been able to explain convincingly to the satisfaction of the PAC why the beneficial effects of agency status could not have been achieved while the VI was still part of the Department of Transport.

The PAC recommended that the department should review whether there was scope for removing some of the constraints under which the agency operated, including the 'rule' that vehicle operators should not have to travel more than 20–30 miles to a testing station, which resulted in assets – testing stations – being underutilized. The PAC suggested that 'customers' be surveyed to see whether they would welcome cheaper fees for testing as a quid pro quo for having to travel further for such tests. (In fact the cost of travel to a testing station for each customer averages around £150 and the fee for testing ranges between £17 and £34, so reducing the fee would be unlikely to have an effect on customers, while increasing the journey to the testing stations might well do.)

The PAC expressed surprise that 'customer service targets have not been set in terms of outputs at all' (*ibid.*: vi). (It is not clear whether this had come about because the agency had been established and its framework document drafted before the Citizen's Charter (1991) had focused on customer satisfaction. In other words, the point may illustrate how the agency initiative forms part of an evolving process of change in public services, the VI giving a snapshot of an agency established at an early stage in that process.) It is noteworthy that in March 1994, in line with the Citizen's Charter and taking up this point, the VI published codes of practice on testing, enforcement and the MOT scheme, which set out customer service standards for the main areas of VI's work and make firm commitments on openness, publication of standards, consultation with trade bodies and the handling of complaints (*Next Steps Review*, 1994).

As far as targets were concerned, the NAO Report showed that there were certain targets or objectives that had been set by the department, and others that had been devised by the agency itself. It emerged that these latter targets had been set largely to reflect what the agency had previously been able to achieve. The PAC felt that these ought to be more challenging, and that performance against them as against departmental targets should be monitored on a continuing basis by the department. On this the Treasury, the agency and the department all disagreed with the PAC.

The PAC report drew a Treasury Minute in response to some of the points, which was defensive of the arrangements. It reads rather like advocacy both for the department and for the agency. The Minute stated that a customer survey was being conducted by the VI as part of its review of the clarity and availability of material about its services, in response to the Citizen's Charter initiative. It maintained that the transfer to agency status provided a powerful impetus for change. As far as the pattern of testing stations – the 20–30-mile 'rule' – was concerned, this was a matter of ministerial policy rather than a 'rule' and, significantly, the Minute stated that: 'The Inspectorate is free to propose changes to the network at any time.' But, it stated, these would be considered by ministers on a case-by-case basis, the view of local customers being taken into account. This is now happening. (The VI is also exploring ways of making testing available at other sites which are capable of carrying out the work, and this is likely to lead to over fifty new testing sites becoming available, and should reduce some journeys to tests.)

The department and the inspectorate were, the Minute records, currently working towards the introduction of output-based perform-ance measures. (It is not easy to produce service measures that are related to objectives and targets that do not distort business.) It was not departmental policy to interfere with internally set targets or objectives. The VI had investigated why four of their objectives were not met, reported on the reasons, and proposed remedial action to its Advisory Board and the department. Action had been taken in the form of extra guidance, training and information, and procedures had been put in place to ensure that the risk of missing objectives was identified early enough for remedial action to be taken 'in-year'.

HER MAJESTY'S STATIONERY OFFICE

HMSO was established in 1786 for the supply of stationery to public offices. Its responsibilities grew to include print buying, printing, publishing and the supply and servicing of office machinery to public bodies. The government decided to privatize most of HMSO in 1996, but retaining a residual body entitled 'HMSO' as a public body, to administor Crown copyright and fulfil certain statutory responsibilities and oversight of the Gazettes. The residual body would also administor parliamentary copyright if either of the two Houses of Parliament so wished. This case study is primarily an accent of the background to the taking of the decision to privatize (HC Deb., vol. 264, cols 370–1w).

Before privatization a large part of the annual turnover of HMSO came from business supplies – stationery and office supplies to govern-ment departments and other public bodies, which used to be vote-funded. About £100 million came from office supplies, £110 million from office equipment to public bodies (HMSO negotiated competitive terms for the renting and servicing of photocopiers, etc.), and some £150 million from printing and publishing. Here it maintained its monopoly role as publisher (although not necessarily as printer) of parliamentary publications, as the Queen's Printer of Acts of Parlia-ment, and as administrator of Crown and parliamentary copyright: hence its most important function was printing and publishing for the Houses of Parliament. (Since the Copyright, Designs and Patents Act 1988, there has been a distinction between documents subject to Crown copyright and those subject to parliamentary copyright. HMSO was the publisher for both.) But HMSO had many other printing functions within goverment, such as the production of passports, forms, booklets and other documents. Where it subcontracted the printing to the private sector, HMSO 'added value' by taking on the design, etc., of the product. Approximately 80 per cent of HMSO's goods and services were procured from the private sector.

HMSO determined its own pricing policy, and its general approach was that it should not cross-subsidize its products except for commercial reasons. In practice, those with whom it contracted were able to influence pricing (one notable instance was the two Houses of Parliament, which adopted a proactive role in their relations with HMSO in the last year or two of its existence). Subject to that possibility, pricing policy is no longer in practice a matter for ministers, so that non-commercial public interest considerations were not imposed on HMSO – for instance in relation to the pricing of Hansard (see Lester *et al.*, 1994; Hansard Society Commission on the Legislative Process, 1992; HL Deb., 14 December 1994: col. 1296).

For HMSO, the last fifteen years or so saw a succession of changes and increasing pressures to operate competitively. In 1982 the government established the Central Unit on Purchasing. This unit put pressure on HMSO to be more competitive by removing its monopoly in relation to government purchasing. Until then exchequer departments were required to purchase from HMSO, but thereafter they had choice as to where to purchase. Some of these changes were regarded as threatening initially, but in practice the combination of 'accountability and freedom' which staff saw in the changes was welcomed and whetted the organization's appetite for freedom in its operations. The introduction of staff recruited from the private sector came to be viewed as positive and creating 'productive tension' by the career civil servants employed there, and was not seen to undermine the public service ethos. The culture of the organization changed under the 'ratchet' effect of the changes, and it sought to respond constructively to them. Relationships with the trade unions became more open, and there was an increased willingness on their part to acknowledge the commercial environment in which the agency operated.

After HMSO was launched as an executive agency in December 1988, its organizational structure was streamlined, some management layers were eliminated, and Civil Service pay and grading were abandoned in 1990. Pay related to the job, and pay progression for the individual was dependent on attaining key targets related to business results. A total quality management (TQM) methodology was adopted, and a business process analysis and redesign process was being undertaken in 1995. Electronic trading was introduced.

As far as the corporate arrangements are concerned the centre is being reduced from 450 staff to some 100 by the end of 1997, and business directors were being appointed to thirteen free-standing business units (for instance, office supplies, copiers, furniture, parliamentary publishing, book sales and service).

Relationships with the Department

Ministerial responsibility for HMSO was transferred from the Treasury to the Chancellor of the Duchy of Lancaster in June 1992. In practice, its contacts pending privatization were with the Parliamentary Secretary of the Office of Public Service and Science (OPSS) and the Permanent Secretary in that office.

The relationship of HMSO with its minister and senior officials in OPSS was a close one. The agency remained accountable to its minister in the established way, but accountability was more transparent because of the use of performance targets and business plans against which performance could be judged. HMSO's perception of its relationship with its minister and its accountability were still strongly imbued with the traditional public service ethos – most of its staff were career civil servants, but the influx of outsiders was seen to be beneficial and not destructive of that ethos.

Financial and Auditing Arrangements

For most of its history, HMSO charged the cost of its services to an 'allied service' vote, but the Treasury (to which it was accountable at the time) decided in the late 1970s that departments should assume full accountability through repayment for goods and services supplied by HMSO. The allied service vote to the two Houses of Parliament was not abolished until 1992, after which subsidies for, for instance, the price of Hansard were withdrawn and pricing was for the House of Commons Commission (or the equivalent body in the Lords) to decide in negotiation with HMSO, rather than for ministers (see HC Deb., 3 April 1995: vol. 257, col. 1502; HL Deb., 17 May 1995: vol. 564, col. 37).

HMSO became a trading fund in 1980, and under its Trading Fund Order (SI 1980/456) its remit was to provide services for public service departments. At the time of the establishment of the trading fund, most of HMSO business was with government departments and the NHS. Thereafter it started to service more of the public sector, including local authorities, universities and, latterly, Members of the European Parliament (MEPs) under a small special vote. HMSO's profit or 'current cost surplus' was used for investment in the office's operations. As a trading fund, HMSO had running costs of £117 million and its turnover was some £354 million in 1995. This was a fall of 10 per cent since 1990. The outstanding original debt was repaid out of profits. Remaining profits were ploughed back into the trading fund to finance capital investment. It paid interest on any short-term loans but did not pay dividends to government. In 1995, for the first time, HMSO produced a trading deficit of £11.6 million before exceptional items, at a time when its financial target had been £11.6 million surplus. The net deficit was taken from reserves (HMSO Trading Fund Account, 1995).

HMSO was involved in 'market testing' for at least fifteen years, but the policy became an explicit and general policy of government from 1993 (*Competing for Quality*, 1993). A consideration in market testing was the problems in providing public access to supplies of public information – annual reports and accounts of public bodies, for instance – which would arise if it were to be published by bodies other than HMSO.

Performance in market tests gives some indication of the value for money HMSO provided. The HMSO Parliamentary Press succeeded in retaining the production of Hansard in the market test for that work in 1994. Its Manchester Press won the lion's share of the UK Passport Agency test for the production of UK passports (HMSO had always produced passports, but had agreed that this should be market tested).

Other 'wins' were with the Scottish Office for design, print and publishing services and the Recruitment and Assessment Services Agency for reprographics. In 1995 HMSO was managing three reprographics units for the DoE. It was estimated in the 1994 *Next Steps Review* that, once implementation was completed, market testing of HMSO services would result in annual savings for its customers in excess of £3 million.

The Review Process

From 1993 to 1995, HMSO was undergoing its third review in seven years. The first had taken place in 1988 when agency status was being considered, and the second took place in 1991. In each of those reviews the conclusion was that HMSO should remain within government, and account was taken of its success in increasing efficiency and making first a return on capital and later a current cost surplus over the years, especially since it received trading-fund status in 1980 and the loss of monopoly in 1982. It had succeeded in reducing costs, adjusting to the commercial environment in which it was operating, and producing increasing profits.

When the third review was started in 1993, it was a 'prior options' review under the government programme *Competing for Quality*, which required consideration to be given expressly to the options of abolition, further commercialization in the public sector, and privatization.

HMSO commissioned BDO Consultants to produce a commercialization study, which identified six possible options, ranging from abolition to various forms of privatization – selling off as one enterprise, or breaking up and selling off parts separately. The BDO recommendation was that HMSO should not be abolished because it was valuable and provided a service to government. On the other hand it was not proposed that matters should be left as they were, but rather that there should be continued improvement in profit and performance. It was felt that it might not be appropriate to disaggregate or break up the activities of HMSO with a view to selling off parts of it to the trade, as this could be costly in redundancy payments and also reduce competition in the market generally.

While the repeated reviews of HMSO were acknowledged to have been beneficial in some respects in keeping up the pressure for performance, negative effects flowed from the fact that the options of either abolition or breaking up the enterprise were kept alive. For instance, the confidence of suppliers to HMSO was affected when supply contracts were being negotiated, and this affected the terms that HMSO can negotiate (HMSO itself experienced lack of confidence in those it supplied because of the question marks over their future – the effects of uncertainty were widespread). Staff morale too suffered from uncertainty about the future.

Privatization of HMSO

As indicated above, in late 1995 the Chancellor of the Duchy of Lancaster decided that, subject to providing Parliament with assurances about maintaining services, it would privatize all but the Crown copyright and miscellaneous other functions of HMSO by the summer of 1996 (HC Deb., vol. 264, col. 455 and col. 183, 17 October 1995). The Chancellor stressed his preference for a sale as a going concern to a financial institution, so as to maintain the integrity and independence of HMSO. The Cabinet Office appointed Coopers and Lybrand to assist with the sale. In the run up to privatization HMSO's relationship with each House of Parliament in the printing and publication of parliamentary papers changed. HMSO entered into supply and service agreements with each House, more formal than previous arrangements, from January 1996. It was anticipated that on privatization, a full contract with legal force would be entered into between the Corporate Officer of each House and the privatized Stationery Office. This would, among other things, make provision for the pricing of Hansard, which HMSO had reduced and pegged in 1991 (HL Deb., vol. 568, cols 712–16). (HC Deb., vol. 268, col. 989, 13 December 1995; HC Deb., vol. 268, col. 1272, 18 December 1995).

THE EMPLOYMENT SERVICE

The aim of the Employment Service as stated in its framework document is 'to promote a competitive, efficient and flexible labour market by helping into work unemployed people, especially those who are disadvantaged, and by paying benefits and allowances to those who are entitled to them'. The objectives, summarized, are:

- to offer unemployed people help and advice in finding work or appropriate training;
- to advise them about their entitlement, etc. in relation to benefits or allowances;
- to offer particular help and advice to people with disabilities;
- to investigate and take action on benefit fraud;
- to provide service in accordance with the Jobseeker's Charter;
- to manage its services efficiently, effectively and economically.

The Employment Service was established in April 1990. At that time it was the largest agency to have been launched in the programme. It employed about 35,000 people and operated a network of over 1600 local offices, mainly jobcentres or unemployment benefit offices. It had an administration and programmes budget of £860 million, and £2.6 billion was paid annually in benefits on behalf of the DSS. Since its establishment there has been an increase in unemployment, and, in accordance with government policy, jobcentres and unemployment benefit offices have been combined. The upshot is that at the end of 1994 the service employed 45,000 staff and had some 1100 local offices. For 1993–4, its overall running costs budget was £1154 million.

The Chief Executive of the Employment Service, Mike Fogden, was an internal appointee when the agency was originally set up. He had been Under-Secretary in the Manpower Policy Division of the DoE, and had effectively been doing the job of running the activities of the Employment Service before it was established as an agency. The work of the agency is highly politically sensitive, and this may account for the fact that the first Chief Executive was an in-house appointee. At the time of the review of the first framework document, the Chief Executive was reappointed for a fixed term after an open competition for the post. A proportion of his pay is determined in the light of the agency's performance.

The staff of the agency remain civil servants, but the Chief Executive has delegated responsibility for pay and systems, recruitment and retention, and other matters. He is responsible for the creation, number and grading of posts up to and including Grade 6, though proposals for new posts at Grade 5 must be approved by the Permanent Secretary and the Secretary of State, and posts above Grade 5 additionally by the Treasury.

Relationships with Departments

Relationships between the Employment Service, the Secretary of State and the parent department are very close, with frequent contact. Although the agency moved into new accommodation outside the DoE when it was formed – a matter of symbolic significance – weekly informal meetings take place with the ministers and 'the top of the office', that is, the Permanent Secretary, the three Deputy Secretaries and junior ministers. These meetings have been taking place since 1987, before the agency was established. These weekly meetings last about an hour; there are no papers or agendas, but they provide opportunities to the parties to raise issues, and for the Chief Executive to draw matters to the attention of the Secretary of State, many of which may be politically sensitive. In addition to this weekly 'prayer meeting' there are one or two formal meetings each week with ministers and/or senior members of the department to consider aspects of the work of the service, and there may be more meetings during the Public Expenditure Survey. There are also meetings quarterly with ministers to review the performance of the service.

The Secretary of State for Employment is responsible for certain elements of the delivery of benefits for unemployment on behalf of the Secretary of State for Social Security; those arrangements are set out and published in *Benefits for Unemployed People*, an agreement between the secretaries of state which they may update independently of the framework document. The Employment Service acts for the Secretary of State in relation to functions described in that agreement.

The Framework Document

The principal agency document is the framework document. (Copies of the framework document and supporting documents and any subsequent revisions agreed by the Secretary of State are placed in the library of both Houses of Parliament.) The framework document is regarded by the Chief Executive as a 'powerful tool' in his hands. Its existence and content have altered radically the relationship between the Chief Executive and the Secretary of State. It is an 'operating memorandum' which enables the Chief Executive to challenge constraints that the department might wish to place on the agency.

For instance, para. 5.11 provides that the Chief Executive's responsibilities in respect of the people who work in the agency include, *inter alia*, 'developing appropriate pay arrangements', a phrase loaded with significance in devolving power to the Chief Executive. Para. 3.12

provides that the Permanent Secretary 'consults the Chief Executive before any policy proposals affecting the agency are put to the Secretary of State'. And by para. 3.3, the Secretary of State may seek advice or information from the Chief Executive on any matter to do with the agency, but does not normally intervene in its day-to-day work.

Under para. 3.8:

> The Chief Executive may make proposals to the Secretary of State for changes in the policies and programmes operated by the Agency, consulting the Permanent Secretary of the Employment Department Group to ensure that they are consistent with the overall policy objectives of the Group. The Chief Executive is a member of the appropiate senior Employment Department Group committees and in that capacity participates in discussions about its overall policy.

It can be seen that these proposals erect barriers against departmental interference, for instance in the day-to-day work of the agency, and enable the Chief Executive to cross barriers that might be expected to be raised against involvement in policy-making matters.

The Employment Service does not fit the pure dogma of the executive agency model because employment policy is highly political, the state of the labour market varies across the country, and in practice the Employment Service knows more about what is happening than the department does.

The first framework document of 1990 was revised and replaced by a second from October 1993. This document will be formally reviewed by March 1997, but the Secretary of State or the Chief Executive may propose modifications at any time. In the course of the 1993 review the Chief Executive found that some attempts were made to constrain some of the managerial and financial flexibilities granted under the first framework document, for instance on matters of finance and personnel (para. 5.11): the position remains that the Chief Executive requires the permission of the Permanent Secretary for appointments to Grade 5.

Both the Treasury and the department were involved in the review, though the Treasury was content to retain the status quo given the satisfactory record of the service in performance delivery. The sorts of issue that arose were to do with the provision of performance information: the service provides information quarterly and fought a successful battle not to be required to provide the information monthly. Another issue was the setting of targets: under the first framework document targets were national, and determination of targets for individual regions was the Chief Executive's own responsibility: he successfully resisted pressure to include regional targets in the revised framework document. Generally the sense is that the Chief Executive (like those in comparable positions in the corporate sector) has to be vigilant in defending his boundaries against incursions from above – the Treasury or the department.

Although Next Steps agencies are meant to be concerned essentially with administrative or operational matters, rather than with policy, in practice these functions – and responsibility for them – cannot be separated by a watertight bulkhead. Thus, while conventional constitutional doctrine may hold that policy is a matter for ministers, taking advice from senior civil servants, as we have seen the framework document provides that the Chief Executive has the right to make proposals to the Secretary of State for changes in the policies and programmes operated by the agency, consulting the Permanent Secretary of the Employment Department Group to ensure that they are consistent with the overall policy objectives of the group. This provides a useful example of how agencies do not necessarily separate policy from administration: what they do is to separate ministers as political policy makers from others.

The Annual Performance Agreement

The Secretary of State and the Chief Executive review and agree each year standards and targets relating to the achievement of the agency's objectives. In the annual performance agreement, the Secretary of State states the resources allocated to the agency, and for each objective sets the targets against which the agency's achievements will be assessed. The agreement also describes supporting information required to set these achievements in context. As described in the framework document this does not sound like an 'agreement', but in practice it results from a process of negotiation between the Secretary of State and the Chief Executive.

The annual performance agreement for 1993–4 illustrates the nature of the exercise. It provided for a gross total of £1392.8 million to be made available to the agency. It set out that the Secretary of State had asked the Employment Service to continue to improve the standard of service it offers its clients in accordance with Citizen's Charter principles and the expectations of its clients. It contained 'performance requirements'. These included a target of 1.47 million placings of unemployed people into work at a planned unit cost of between £204.90 and £226, assuming 2.05–2.15 million vacancies were notified; 27 per cent of total unemployed placings achieved to be long-term claimants; and so on. And it set out what supporting information was to be provided.

By way of illustration of the review process, in the autumn of each year the number and nature of target areas are settled between the agency and the department. On the basis of these, in January, discussions take place with the department about volume for the coming year. These discussions have to consider a range of possibilities, and eventually agreement should be reached with the Permanent Secretary or Deputy Secretary and then with the Secretary of State. Agreement then has to be reached with the DSS, since the Employment Service delivers some benefits for that department. The Chief Secretary to the Treasury has to be satisfied that the Secretary of State has set sufficiently stretching and meaningful targets, which should be challenging but realistic. Once the annual targets are set between the service and the department, the agency determines internally its regional targets by discussion with its regional directors.

The 1994 *Next Steps Review* indicated that the Employment Service had achieved most of its targets and exceeded some, though it was operating in the context of better labour market conditions, which were not of course of its making. The targets it failed to achieve were missed by only about 0.1 per cent. The targets for 1994–5 were refined to take account of performance, market conditions and pressures for efficiency savings, and in some cases increased. For the most part these were met and exceeded (*Next Steps Review*, 1995).

Once the annual performance agreement has been drawn up, the Employment Service produces its own operational plan. This sets out how the agency proposes to meet the performance requirements contained in the annual agreement. The operational plan is a much more detailed document than either of the other two. Under this plan, which is subject to approval by the Secretary of State, the Chief Executive undertakes to maintain the programmes and services described in the performance agreement. It sets out how the agency proposes to secure value for money, its procurement policy, its market testing programme, its research and evaluation plans, and how it plans to meet its aim and objectives and targets. For instance, for 1993–4, it set itself the target that 87 per cent of first payments of benefit were to be dispatched on the day that entitlement to benefit was established, rising to 90 per cent by the year end. As far as personnel matters are concerned, the 1993–4 plan stated that there would be negotiation with the trade union side about various changes, including those to key contractual terms such as the policies and procedures governing discipline, inefficiency and grievance. There were to be revised arrangements for performance pay for certain grades, which linked rewards more closely with individual levels of performance and the demands of particular jobs.

The Chief Executive also undertakes to provide the Secretary of State with a full report on the agency's performance and use of resources within a given time of the end from the year to which the agreement relates. There is provision for the Chief Executive to provide monthly profiles of expenditure by vote subject, and a quarterly report concerning prescribed information.

The Advisory Group

In 1993 the Chief Executive set up an advisory group of people from outside the Employment Service to whom he would look for an external perspective on issues affecting the development of the Agency. The group meets bimonthly, and papers are prepared in advance indicating the matters on which advice is sought. The members are drawn from the private sector and, in one case, from the Institute for Employment Research at the University of Warwick.

The Chief Executive resisted suggestions that non-executive directors should be appointed, or a departmental group, since the need he perceived was for a focus group of people recruited from analogous operations in the private sector. Hence the members include one from a high street banking chain, a high street retailer, a former financial director of a computer company, and one person with a background in management consultancy. The group does not include a 'representative' from the clients of the Employment Service – for instance, someone involved in one of the voluntary groups operating in this area – as the Chief Executive felt that the interests and views of clients could be better taken into account through national customer satisfaction surveys, which the service has commissioned for five years, and local surveys.

There was also a perception that the inclusion of client representatives in the administrative boards in Sweden is part of the social partnership model, which has been strong in Sweden but not in England. Most of the pressure groups involved in this field were seen as advocates of particular causes, who might feel compromised if included in the group. No complaints had been received about the fact that clients were not represented in any way on the group.

Financial and Auditing Arrangements

The Chief Executive of the Employment Service has been appointed by the Treasury as additional accounting officer for the Employment Service, with responsibility for the agency's vote, covering administrative, capital and programme expenditure. Many of the financial arrangements for the agency are set out in the *Memorandum of Financial Arrangements* published by the Employment Department. This is the text of an agreement between the Permanent Secretary of the Employment Department Group and the Chief Executive. It recites that the framework document delegates responsibility for managing the agency to the Chief Executive, and the memorandum describes the detailed practical arrangements to implement the financial aspects of the framework document.

The agency's resources are determined annually as part of the Employment Department Group Public Expenditure Survey (PES) settlement. The Chief Executive is responsible for seeking the resources he needs to manage the agency. The agency submits PES and estimates requirements to the department with explanatory information, sets out its priorities and planning assumptions, provides additional supporting material as requested, and participates in discussions with the Treasury on specific PES and estimates requirements.

Following the annual allocation of resources, the Chief Executive consults the department and advises the Secretary of State on any changes to the operation of agreed policy or procedures which might be necessary as a result of the allocation. The Chief Executive decides the distribution of resources within the agency, subject to consultation with the department if there are wider consequences for the Employment Department Group. He draws up a pay negotiating remit within the paybill control total, and consults the department. The agency submits financial out-turn and staffing reports to the department. The Chief Executive reports progress quarterly towards the achievement of the annual performance agreement and meets with the Secretary of State to discuss performance.

The position is elaborated in the four appendices to the memorandum. There is some virement (i.e. transfer of resources from one funding head to another, within specified limits). 'The presumption is that Treasury approval for virement within the terms of the guidelines will normally be given, although formal confirmation of this will need to be obtained' (Appendix 1). The agency may undertake activities which generate revenue in accordance with guidelines in Appendix 3 to the memorandum. For example, employers and others may be charged for agency activities, but jobseekers will not be charged for any employment-related activities undertaken. There are provisions on VFM, financial authorities, and the right to carry forward into the next financial year certain unspent moneys.

In addition to the mechanisms provided for under the Executive Agency arrangements and the Citizen's Charter (see below), the performance of the agency is subject to normal methods of audit of various kinds – internal monitoring, external audit and scrutiny for financial propriety from the Department of Employment, the Treasury, the Comptroller and Auditor General, the NAO and ultimately the PAC. It is also liable to be subjected to audit for efficiency and effectiveness in meeting the targets set out at various levels of particularity in the array of agency documents from various of these bodies, and from the Select

Committee for Employment should it wish to conduct such an inquiry.

Relationships with Parliament

The framework document provides that 'When a Parliamentary Committee wants to take evidence about the operations of the agency, the Secretary of State will normally ask the Chief Executive to represent him' (para. 3.5). On a number of occasions, select committees of the House of Commons have considered the activities of the Employment Service, and the Chief Executive appeared before the TCSC in 1991 (TCSC, Seventh Report, 1991), the Employment Select Committee in 1992 (*Employment Committee*, 1993), the PAC on a number of occasions and in 1995 the Select Committee for the PCA (see below).

In practice the Chief Executive feels that he can often be more robust in these appearances than when he was an Under-Secretary in the department. He accepts the conventional position that he may not criticize ministerial policy and he would, if pressed, draw attention to the fact that he was implementing explicit policy and indicate that questions about that policy should be directed to the minister. But he might feel able to indicate, for instance, that the targets were too stretching in relation to the resources given, if that were the case.

The feeling about appearance before select committees seems to be one of strong identification with the department, despite the separation of the agency from the main department. The analogy was drawn of the relationship between a managing director and a chairperson of a company board of directors: it would not be considered appropriate for the Chief Executive to criticize the minister at a committee hearing any more than it would be for a managing director to criticize the chair at a shareholders' meeting.

As far as dealing with written parliamentary questions and individual letters about matters which the Secretary of State has delegated to the Chief Executive is concerned, in accordance with the recommendation of the Select Committee on Procedure (Third Report, 1990–1: paras. 122–6) as accepted by the House (HC Deb., 20 October 1992: vol. 212, col. 289), the framework document states that the Chief Executive's replies to parliamentary questions will be published in the *Official Report*. These questions currently number about two hundred and fifty a year, and for the most part they are requests for information and do not raise individual constituents' grievances.

MPs, MEPs and the public are encouraged to write direct to the Chief Executive or other appropriate agency manager on individual cases, or operational issues. But, according to the framework document, 'Matters of concern may also be raised with the Secretary of State, particularly if the issue is not resolved satisfactorily through correspondence with the Chief Executive' (para. 3.4). The Chief Executive receives about 1500 such letters from MPs in a year. Only rarely have MPs not been satisfied with the response and raised the question with the Secretary of State. There has been no suggestion that a lay adjudicator or agency ombudsman on the lines of the Revenue Adjudicator should be appointed. The agency has an in-house compensation scheme under its internal complaints procedure, and clients have access to the Adjudication Authorities and Tribunals in case of complaints about eligibility for benefits.

The Citizen's Charter and the Employment Service

The Citizen's Charter is regarded by the Chief Executive as a very important part of the agency concept which should improve standards of service to the public, capture the commitment of those working in the organization, and produce better value for the taxpayer's money. There is a high level of satisfaction in the service with recognition of its successes in these objectives, for instance in winning the Civil Service competition to identify good customer service; the agency obtained 'Investors in People' status in 1995 for its policies for the development of those working in the organization. Three of its offices obtained charter marks. Several annual awards have been received for the plain English of some of its publications.

The Jobseeker's Charter was first issued in December 1991, updated in May and September 1993, revised in 1994 and reprinted in 1995 to include 1994–5 performance information. A new charter for jobseekers is to be published in 1996, in consultation with the Benefits Agency. This charter sets out the help and standards of service that the agency's clients can expect. This is agreed by the Secretary of State and published by the agency; it is supplemented in turn by a booklet entitled 'Just the Job', giving more information about the assistance provided to jobseekers by the Employment Service. The charter itself contains procedural 'guarantees' of a personal interview, help in drawing up a 'back to work' plan, and polite and considerate treatment by staff. It promises to make available information about entitlement to unemployment benefit and other benefits and about the standards of service in local offices and the results they achieve. It also promises advice on matters such as employment and training opportunities, and support in the form of opportunities such as a job interview guarantee, employment training, and restart courses for those who are unemployed after six months. The charter includes a tear-off slip about how to complain or make suggestions. The service received some 8000 complaints in the first quarter of

1995, 7000 'compliments', and 250 suggestions as to the ways in which services could be improved.

The charter is not only about what the client can expect of the agency, but also about the duties of the client – to be available for and actively seek work, follow through steps agreed in the 'back to work' plan, go to interviews arranged with employers, keep appointments, and inform the jobcentre of changes of address and circumstances, such as starting work.

According to the *Citizen's Charter Second Report* (1994), achievements under the charter initiative have included the insertion of a clause on meeting charter standards in contracts with programme providers (an example of the use of contract to promote policies that have no independent legal force). By April 1995 90 per cent of jobcentres and unemployment benefit offices had been integrated, computerized queue management systems are operating in offices, information about jobs is displayed on Teletext, and automatic credit transfer is available instead of girocheques to all recipients of unemployment benefit. Moreover, annual customer satisfaction surveys are carried out and the results published, and coordination between the Benefits Agency and the Employment Service is being improved on the basis of a joint task force's recommendations.

Relationships with the PCA and the Select Committee

The agency has had problems in dealings with the PCA and his Select Committee. These culminated in an appearance by the Chief Executive before the committee in May 1995 in which he had to answer some very probing questions and deal with strong criticism (*Fourth Report of the Select Committee of the Parliamentary Commissioner for Adminstration*, HC 394, 1994–5).

The PCA had raised with the Select Committee the question of delay in three cases involving the Employment Service at the stages when his investigations were complete and his draft report had been sent to the service so that factual accuracy could be checked and redress offered. Delays had amounted to twelve months, four months and ten months respectively in these cases.

The committee felt, and the Chief Executive agreed, that such delays were not acceptable. It emerged that the Chief Executive had been, as he put it, 'over-protective' of his staff, had viewed the PCA as representing the complainant against the agency, and felt that the agency's voice was not being heard or that what they were saying was not being given the same weight as for the complainants. He had thus been fending off the

PCA. The Select Committee stressed that they would be disturbed if the PCA appeared to be adopting solely the stance of the complainant, without due care and consideration for the operations of staff in a department in respect of which a complaint was being investigated. Here we have a rejection of the ombudsman as a 'citizen's defender', which is how the office is viewed in some countries. The committee insisted that the Chief Executive was personally responsible for dealing with complaints from the ombudsman and should not leave it to local officials to do so; he was also personally responsible, they insisted, for making sure that complaints systems in the organization were operating effectively.

It also emerged in the Chief Executive's evidence to the Select Committee that the agency's reaction to the PCA's report had been influenced by the fact that, under the agency arrangements, the service was very much performance-driven and cost-driven. Those pressures mean that staff feel that they are under a duty to deliver government policy as expressed in the regulations; for instance, regulations require claimants to be actively seeking work, as opposed to being available for work, since 1989. This pressure and set of attitudes produce, in the Chief Executive's words, a 'slightly ambiguous agenda', 'a mixture of welfare and warfare', and foster an antagonistic interface between agency staff and their 'clients' (HC 394, 1994–5: p. 22, para. 119).

The committee felt that the problem was more attitudinal than functional and urged a change of attitude, noting that the same attitude did not prevail in the DSS and its agencies, where similar pressures operate. They felt a change of attitude in the agency was particularly necessary since, in the following year (1996), the agency would be responsible for administering the proposed new 'jobseeker's allowance', which could well give rise to very severe transitional problems and risked the sort of crisis that had arisen in the CSA (see Chapter 1).

The Chief Executive was pressed by the committee to express a view about the arrangements proposed by the minister for the introduction of the new allowance. His responses illustrate the difficulties created by the traditional or cultural reticence about criticizing the minister:

There is a range of views as to the mechanisms that are being put in place. My job is to make the mechanism that has been put in place and decided by the Government work. That is my professional position. We will make it work . . . There was a range of administrative solutions for developing and introducing the jobseeker's allowance and naturally enough, as you would expect, I have views about each of those various options. The Government has decided the way that they want the

jobseekeer's allowance to be introduced and I will make sure
that it is introduced. (para. 126)

He was then asked directly: 'Is [this arrangement] the one that you
would have preferred?'. His reply was: 'Instinctively the answer has to
be no' (para. 128).

Members of the Select Committee expressed strong concern about the
proposed arrangements: 'You are in charge of an agency which may well
be going the wrong way' (para. 129). They urged him to delay if
necessary rather than allow the same mistakes as the CSA had made to
be repeated. To this the Chief Executive replied: 'I am sure that all of us
in public administration are scarred by the experience of the Child
Support Agency and we will ensure that there will not be a repetition
irrespective of whatever the administrative arrangements that we have'
(para. 129).

Among the committee's recommendations to the Chief Executive
during his appearance were that there should be no further delays in
dealing with PCA draft reports, and that he should personally involve
himself in those cases. The committee also recommended that the whole
complaints investigation procedure be tightened up, that attitudes to
'clients' be improved so that the relationship with clients be more
'emollient', that staff be informed by a circular about the role of the
ombudsman, that very careful preparations be made for the introduction of the jobseeker's allowance, and that the committee be assured in
due course that staff are properly trained in the operation of the open
government code.

The Employment Service's relationship with the PCA also illustrates
the PCA's jurisdiction over privatized services. The PCA investigated a
complaint in 1995 about the contracting out of Jobclubs. Contracts
take the form of agreements with the Secretary of State whereby the
provider establishes and runs a Jobclub in accordance with the provisions of the agreement and in a manner acceptable to the Department.
The Jobseekers' Charter provides for a complaints procedure that
extends to Jobclubs. A complainant alleged that the ES had failed to take
effective action to remedy an injustice he claimed to have suffered when
he was excluded from a Jobclub by an external provider. The PCA found
that the expulsion had been within the terms of the provider's contract,
but he had some concerns about the way in which the case had been
dealt with. He requested the Chief Executive to ensure that appropriate
compensation arrangements are made when, although there has been no
error on the part of the Employment Service, maladministration by a
contractor has caused a Jobclub member actual financial loss. The Chief
Executive also agreed to tighten the contract clause requiring providers

to make a report on each expulsion so as to specify the format and timing of such reports (PCA Annual Report for 1995, para. 49).

CONCLUSIONS

It is not possible to say with confidence that the subjects of these case studies are representative of how the agencies are operating across the board, but they do illustrate some characteristics of the initiative and provide some evidence for general lessons to be drawn from experience of the Next Steps initiative and the Citizen's Charter.

We can see that the changes in the climate in which executive agencies operate have been taking place for at least fifteen years, and have had a 'ratchet' effect. The trading-fund arrangements, ideas like the introduction of the Central Unit for Purchasing, the establishment of activities as executive agencies, the market testing programme and prior options reviews have run together as a developing process of commercialization which, though regarded as threatening by some at first, came to be regarded as providing opportunities and increasing freedom for management. Generally the changes, which are seen by the agencies as combining freedom with accountability, have operated to improve not only performance and concern about the individual customer but also profitability, and they have resulted in much more flexible and specialist corporate structures and working relationships with devolved responsibility. Ultimately, as with HMSO, they can lead to privatization.

A strong sense of loyalty to the department was found in all three agencies, with an acceptance of the conventions of ministerial responsibility, in the sense of loyalty to the parent department and minister and willingness to try to work within traditional parameters governing the allocation of responsibility. Chief executives in all three agencies accepted the constraints imposed by *Departmental Evidence and Response to Select Committees* (1994), which on some views correspond closely to conventions operating in the private sector about relations between chairs of enterprises and managing directors.

The Next Steps arrangements were very strongly welcomed by the management in these three agencies and were seen as logical developments from earlier reforms. If anything, chief executives would have liked to see increased delegation to them of managerial power, while they also accepted the relationships between the department and the agency. The psychological impact of the arrangements on organizations was felt to be important within the agencies, though it has not always been apparent to the PAC. The arrangements have evidently improved the corporate spirit within agencies, and the Citizen's Charter arrangements for public recognition of achievement, for instance through the charter mark, have been appreciated on a local level despite some national scepticism about the value of these mechanisms. As far as performance is concerned, there seems to be a general view that this has improved in respect of both VFM and customer services.

Experience of the first few years of operation of the three agencies indicates that the arrangements can heighten the transparency both of what the agency is supposed to be doing and of the department's code, and hence increase the accountability of both to the NAO, to the Comptroller and Auditor General and, via the PAC, to the House of Commons. Agencies will also be more accountable to their departments as objectives are more clearly defined so that performance can be measured against them.

The case studies indicate too that the departments are made accountable by the arrangements to the agency and to the broader public and Parliament, since it will be clearer than in pre-agency days when departmental policy limits the ability of an agency to obtain a full return on its assets; or when departmental restrictions on entrepreneurial activity limit the income-generation capacity of the agency. That sort of clarity, together with the opportunity for the chief executive to propose changes in policy or *ad hoc* changes, can pave the way for pressure to be brought to bear on departments to justify and to reconsider their policy in a way that would have been unlikely to happen under the old arrangements.

Overall, the responsibilities of the agencies are much clearer under the trading-fund and agency arrangements than previously. Accountability is many-sided. Through contractual arrangements (e.g. for the production of Hansard) and votes, agencies may be accountable to the Houses of Parliament, as in the HMSO case. Through financial auditing arrangements, agencies are accountable to the PAC, the Treasury, the NAO and the Comptroller and Auditor General. Through other contracting relationships with government departments and those they supply, either with goods and services or 'policy outputs', agencies are under pressure to be responsive because of the market testing policy.

Major problems arise in developing measures of performance, in monitoring them, and in drawing the line between delegation and departmental responsibility. There is scepticism in some quarters as to whether the benefits that have flowed from transfer to agency status could not have been achieved in other ways, though chief executives seem convinced (and in the case of the VI persuaded the NAO) of the 'catalytic' effect of the transfer on attitudes among staff, which could not have been achieved without agency status. Here differences seem to be opening up between different select committees in the House of Commons, which could undermine the collective, corporate ability of the Commons to impose accountability on the agencies. The absence of legislation authorizing the initiative is significant, for it is quite open to one committee – the PAC in this context – to take a highly sceptical line on the initiative while others – the TCSC (now the Public Service Committee), for instance – take another, more sympathetic line.

As we saw in Chapter 1, the effect of these arrangements on ministerial responsibility is a grey area. Some alternatives to ministerial responsibility, in the sense of ministers having the exclusive right to account for activity, are gradually developing. Financial responsibility is the key, so that in trading funds and where chief executives are agency accounting officers, a real concept of chief executives being accountable to Parliament is evolving. Increasingly MPs are dealing directly with chief executives, and generally this arrangement seems to be operating satisfactorily. Where individual grievances are concerned, the internal complaints procedures required under the Citizen's Charter provide safety valves for dissatisfied 'consumers', and access to the PCA provides an effective last resort.

We see in the encounter between the Chief Executive of the Employment Service and the Select Committee on the PCA the pressure that can be imposed on an agency by such committees and the PCA, and the high degree of personal responsibility directly to Parliament that can be demanded in areas such as complaint handling and planning for change.

The agency arrangements have brought to the top of the political agenda questions about the accountability of agencies. The repercussions of problems in the Prison Service and the CSA (see Chapter 1) have meant that ministers are paying greater attention to managerial questions. It seems that select committees will be putting pressure on chief executives too to avoid similar mistakes in future. The responsiveness of agencies and departments and their ministers to complaints about agencies has been increased as reactions to the activities of the PAC and the NAO (in the case of the VI), the PCA and his Select Committee, and other departmental select committees (and general press comment).

We can observe the importance of 'customers' in these arrangements, whether they are in the parent department or in the outside world. This is marked by the shift of emphasis from inputs to outputs and outcomes, the continuing close relationship between agencies and departments, and the use of customer satisfaction surveys, market testing and competition to change staff attitudes. But, as the case of the Employment Service illustrates, there are risks that the pressure on agencies to achieve performance targets can undermine their responsiveness to complaints and findings of maladministration, unless the role of the PCA and the position of the Select Committee on this matter is made clear to all staff in agencies.

Despite concern about the weakening of mechanisms for the redress of grievance under the arrangements, the rules about MPs' correspondence and parliamentary questions seem to operate in a broadly satisfactory way.

The flexibility of the model maximizes adaptation and responsiveness. We have seen, for instance, how the advisory committees or boards can adapt, how relationships can develop, and how framework documents can be altered to meet changing needs.

A major contribution of the agency arrangements, linked to the Citizen's Charter, is that the criteria against which accountability and responsibility are to be imposed are made explicit, whereas previously matters were left to be dealt with under the conventions of ministerial responsibility to Parliament, where there are no explicit criteria, or under those of the responsibility of civil servants to ministers, where, again, there were few explicit criteria against which performance or behaviour could be judged. Here we can observe a process of 'normativization' of relationships in government, which is also to be found in many other areas of government.

8

Cross-National Perspectives: Sweden and New Zealand

We saw in Chapter 2 that the New Public Management Revolution has been an international phenomenon, though the extent and nature of revolutionary change have varied widely from one country to another. Such variations inevitably reflect the diversity of political cultures, economic circumstances and constitutional arrangements in the countries concerned.

In its report on the role of the Civil Service, published in November 1994, the Commons TCSC noted that consideration of public service reform programmes in other countries 'draws attention to the extent to which such reform programmes share common objectives and espouse similar approaches' (TCSC, 1994: HC 27 – I, para. 147). It identified four common elements in these programmes, which are shared with Civil Service reforms in the UK:

- A movement away from preoccupation with inputs and processes, towards a more 'results-orientated' culture. Recent developments in Canada and the USA (notably, Vice-President Gore's National Performance Review) are cited as cases in point.
- Stress on the needs of the individual customer. Denmark, Canada and Australia provide good examples of this.
- Increased delegation to and empowerment of local managers. Canada, Sweden and the USA are cited here.
- Effective and more businesslike management of resources, including innovations such as moves towards more sophisticated accrual-based accounting methods. Developments in the USA, Iceland, New Zealand, Finland and Australia are mentioned by the committee in this context.

Here we examine developments in two other countries – significantly different from one another, and from Britain, and both mentioned in the Select Committee's list. They provide particularly useful comparative benchmarks for our discussion of public service reform in the UK.

Commentators on politics and government in the UK have, in recent years, shown particular interest in drawing comparisons and contrasts between constitutional and administrative arrangements in Britain and those to be found in New Zealand and Sweden. The TCSC noted that, in the evidence it had received, New Zealand's public service reforms had been referred to more than those of any other country. This choice of comparators may seem rather strange, if for no other reason than that of contrasting size, with the combined populations of the countries in question being just over one-fifth of that of the UK. But the fact remains that the comparisons and contrasts between the British system, and the changes it has undergone, and the experiences of the two countries – one a near neighbour, and a recent recruit to the European Union, and the other a Commonwealth country, with a Westminster-style constitution – are particularly illuminating.

Three matters, in particular, have excited curiosity. The first – Sweden's development of an advanced welfare state, supported by high rates of taxation – is on the face of it peripheral to the concerns of this book, and the economic and political rationale of the Swedish welfare system has, in any case, been undergoing a substantial reappraisal in the face of Sweden's economic problems. However, British politicians and social policy analysts continue to be interested in Scandinavian welfare models, particularly in the context of both Sweden and its neighbour, Finland, having joined the enlarged European Union in 1995.

Its relevance to our study is as an important reminder that the political and ideological forces that have driven public sector reform differ widely from country to country: Swedish arrangements and their reform have been prompted by substantially different concerns from the ones that lie behind the New Public Management Revolution in Britain. And this is quite apart from the constitutional differences that must be taken into account in any attempt at cross-national comparison.

The second matter, more germane to our present concerns, is the fact that both Sweden and New Zealand featured prominently in the discussions that led to the adoption in Britain of a parliamentary ombudsman system in the 1960s, and have continued to provide external points of reference for the subsequent extension and diversification of ombudsman machinery in Britain and elsewhere. The development of effective political and legal mechanisms of accountability and redress of grievances is an important issue in any discussion of the implications of the New Public Management Revolution; and the many variations on the ombudsman theme are important in that context.

The third area of comparison is in relation to the substantive content and direction of public sector reform. There are interesting differences as well as similarities between the reform experiences of these two countries and the experience of Britain.

The Fulton Report on the Civil Service, published in 1968, contained proposals for the development of management by objectives in central departments and for an inquiry into the desirability of 'hiving off' departmental functions to independent boards; and the latter proposals, in particular, owed a lot to comparisons drawn from Sweden. These ideas were later to resurface, in new guises, in the reform programmes of the 1980s, and some instructive comparisons – particularly in relation to the Next Steps programme – can be drawn with Swedish arrangements.

As far as New Zealand is concerned, the New Public Management Revolution has in many respects gone much further than it has in Thatcher's and Major's Britain, and developments there have been accompanied by some very interesting constitutional and legal developments – and by some equally interesting problems. The New Zealand experience has recently been applauded, even endorsed as a possible model for future reform, by British commentators, particularly in some of the evidence submitted to the TCSC in its 1992–4 inquiry into the role of the Civil Service.

REDRESS OF GRIEVANCE

But let us first look at developments on the ombudsman front. We have already noted that at the heart of the debate about the consequences of the New Public Management Revolution are concerns with accountability and redress of citizens' grievances about the performance and the quality of public services. As public service functions move out of the ambit of ministerial and political control into semi-detached agencies, contracted-out arrangements and quangos, developing new, more effective methods of accountability becomes an important priority.

Improving and making more accessible the machinery for redress of grievances is, as we saw in Chapter 3, an important feature of the Citizen's Charter – and variations upon the ombudsman theme offer promising lines for such improvement in many contexts. Many ombudsmen, and offices not called by that name but having some of the characteristics of ombudsmen, have been introduced in the United Kingdom (in the private sector as well as in the public sector) since the PCA was established in the 1960s.

THE SWEDISH OMBUDSMAN

The establishment of a parliamentary ombudsman in Sweden at the beginning of the nineteenth century marked the origins of the modern ombudsman movement, which reached the United Kingdom in 1967 with the establishment of the office of PCA. However, the 'movement' in fact moved very little for about one hundred and fifty years: indeed, until Finland established an ombudsman in 1919, Sweden was the only country that had such an office. It was not until the 1950s and 1960s that other countries – Denmark (in 1953); West Germany (a military ombudsman, in 1957); Norway and New Zealand (both 1962); Guyana and Tanzania (both in 1966); and the UK (in 1967) – acquired ombudsman systems. Today there are at least 180 fully-fledged ombudsman systems, operating at different levels of government and in different administrative sectors, throughout the world, and there are several ombudsmen in the UK, operating alongside the PCA. But the Swedish ombudsman is still regarded by many as the benchmark against which other systems are judged.

The word 'ombudsman' is sometimes said to have originated with the early Germanic tribes, as the title given to a person chosen to collect blood money from a wrongdoer on behalf of an aggrieved party. But its modern and more familiar usage comes from Sweden, where the word is in general use to denote an 'entrusted person', a representative or an attorney, and has acquired a more specialized meaning as a 'citizens' defender' (a meaning rejected by the Select Committee for the PCA in their meeting with the Chief Executive of the Employment Service in 1995: see Chapter 7) or an independent investigator of public grievances.

The history of the office of the Swedish parliamentary ombudsman illustrates many of the issues surrounding this institution as it has been exported and adapted round the world. The office dates back to 1809, though it had antecedents in the office of Chancellor of Justice, established in 1713. The latter office – an 'executive ombudsman', who operates from within the administration – still coexists with the parliamentary ombudsmen, who perform a similar role on behalf of the Swedish Parliament, the Riksdag. The Chancellor of Justice tends to be approached less by members of the public than by administrative agencies themselves, seeking an authoritative ruling on the legality of their actions.

In 1809, the Swedish Riksdag adopted a new constitution which provided for the appointment by the king of a chancellor of justice, and for the election by the Riksdag of an ombudsman for justice (Justitieombudsman, commonly abbreviated to JO), who was to be 'a man of known legal ability and outstanding integrity' (the office was not opened to women until 1941). The parliamentary ombudsman's role, exercised on behalf of the Riksdag, was and is to ensure compliance with the law by all state officials and judges. Few other ombudsmen systems include the judiciary within their jurisdiction, and because of sensitivities about judicial independence, the British PCA has only quite recently acquired jurisdiction even in respect of court administrators employed by the Lord Chancellor's Department.

The purpose of the supervision is to ensure 'the application in public service of laws and other statutes', that courts of law and administrative authorities observe the provisions of the constitution concerning objectivity and impartiality, and that the fundamental rights and freedoms of citizens are not encroached upon in the process of public administration. (Lundvik, 1983b). It is worth noting in passing an important contrast between the Swedish ombudsman and the British PCA, as the latter does not have jurisdiction to deal with complaints of illegality.

Originally the Swedish ombudsman's function was that of a special prosecutor of public servants alleged to be at fault, but since 1976 this role has greatly decreased, so that faults other than crimes such as bribery and embezzlement (which are of course amenable to prosecution) are punishable only if the fault was intentional or due to gross negligence and committed in the exercise of public authority. Historically, though, the criminal process has been regarded as an appropriate mechanism for controlling public administration in Sweden, and this has never been the case in Britain save where offences of corruption or dishonesty are alleged.

The office of Swedish parliamentary ombudsman has undergone several important reorganizations since its establishment. In 1915, a separate military ombudsman was established alongside the Ombudsman for Justice; but in 1968, in consequence of the imbalance of workload between the two ombudsmen, the offices were amalgamated, and the Riksdag appointed three ombudsmen under the single institution of Justitieombudsman; further reorganizations occurred in 1975, and again in 1986. There are now four ombudsmen, one of whom is the Chief Ombudsman, who is responsible for the administration and staffing of the office and for the general distribution of responsibilities among himself or herself and his or her colleagues.

The ombudsmen are elected at a plenary session of the Riksdag (a unicameral legislature since 1971) for four-year terms, with the possibility of re-election. There is a convention that the ombudsman must enjoy all-party support within the legislature, and in recent years ombudsmen have been elected by acclamation. It is also a convention that ombudsmen should not be members of the Riksdag. In practice, the ombudsmen are recruited from judicial backgrounds. The case-load of the Swedish ombudsmen nowadays averages about 3000 complaints a year (a not insignificant total for a country whose population is only 8.6 million). More than a third of these are dismissed without investigation, about half produce no formal criticism following an investigation, and only about 12 per cent result in a formal admonition or other criticism of the bodies subject to complaint. These are the main weapons of the ombudsman, who cannot himself or herself annul or correct a decision or require a particular action.

The ombudsman is, as noted earlier, an officer of the Riksdag, and he or she reports to the Riksdag annually. These reports are studied by the Riksdag's Committee on the Constitution, and discussed at a plenary session of the Riksdag. They are considered to be of public importance and are influential. But there is no true equivalent of the House of Commons Select Committee for the PCA, which can examine public officials where criticism is made of their work (see the Employment Service case study, in Chapter 7, for instance).

A major reason for the importance attached to the office of ombudsman in Sweden is that it provides a strong mechanism of public accountability in a system of public administration in which there has always been a sharp dividing line between policy making (the province of ministers) and administration (the responsibility of autonomous administrative boards). The ombudsmen are appointed by the Riksdag; but, unlike their British counterpart, they are directly accessible to members of the public and enjoy wide powers of independent initiative. They control their own case-load rather than having it controlled for them by MPs. Broadly speaking, Swedish ministers, in charge of quite small central ministries, are answerable to the Riksdag for matters of policy; the directors of administrative boards are subject to administrative law and to the wide jurisdiction of a powerful ombudsman.

THE NEW ZEALAND OMBUDSMAN

The appointment of an ombudsman in New Zealand in 1962 was an important factor in overcoming the resistance of sceptics in Britain, who argued that the office was manifestly incompatible with Westminster-style parliamentary government based on ministerial responsibility. Like the PCA in Britain, the New Zealand ombudsman is an officer of Parliament and answerable to Parliament, but there is no MP-filter like that operating in Britain. He or she may deal with complaints that have been made to him or her, or on his or her own initiative, although this latter right has been exercised only sparingly.

The New Zealand ombudsman's competence to make findings and recommendations extends to any administrative decision, recommendation, act or omission which the New Zealand ombudsman judges to be 'unreasonable, unjust, oppressive or improperly discriminatory' or even simply 'wrong'. He or she takes action, for instance, when he or she finds that a discretionary power has been exercised for an improper purpose, on irrelevant grounds, or taking irrelevant considerations into account. These grounds mirror many of those for judicial review (see Chapter 5), thus emphasizing the fact that there is not the limitation in New Zealand that there is in Britain which shuts out the PCA from questions of legality.

Lundvik (1983a) observes that the New Zealand ombudsman has devoted much energy to promoting a good and fair administration based on high standards of morality in the public service, and that this may denote a new element in the history of law.

The jurisdiction extends to local government and state-owned enterprises, and to officers and employees of educational boards and hospital boards. The ombudsman may also recommend that a practice that seems unreasonable, unjust, oppressive or improperly discriminatory should be altered or the law be changed, thus moving beyond the field of redress of individual grievances. We can detect a similar development in the UK with the publication of special PCA reports on *Delays in Handling Disability Living Allowance Claims* (1993) and *Investigation of Complaints against the Child Support Agency* (1995). But the New Zealand ombudsman is not meant to be a citizen's defender in the sense of a critic of individual public servants – on occasions ombudsmen have found it necessary to advise complainants that they should cease groundless attacks on departments or officials (Lundvik, 1983a). Moreover, he or she does not have powers of prosecution, thus maintaining the common law tradition that criminal sanctions are not appropriate for the faults of public officials outside the fields of corruption and dishonesty.

The reply to critics who claimed that an ombudsman is incompatible with ministerial responsibility is that an ombudsman only has the power to recommend, not to decide, and, far from cutting across the convention of ministerial responsibility, he or she can be seen to reinforce the roles both of the constituency representative and of the minister, by adding an extra channel of official accountability over and above the traditional mechanisms already in place. This indeed was the rationale for including an MP–filter in the UK PCA scheme and of making the PCA accountable to the House of Commons via a select committee.

PUBLIC SERVICE REFORM IN THE UK: THE FULTON REPORT AND THE SWEDISH EXAMPLE

The Fulton Committee on the Civil Service was set up in 1966, and the committee began work at almost exactly the same time that the PCA legislation was being debated in Parliament. Its report, published in 1968 (Cmnd 3638), made no reference to the new ombudsman, but it did show considerable interest in Swedish public administration and, in particular, the separation between ministries and boards, noted above.

Chapter 5 of the Fulton Report was entitled, 'The Structure of Departments and the Promotion of Efficiency'. It contained two particularly significant recommendations: first, it advocated the introduction into the Civil Service of management by objectives and of accountable management and, second, it called for an inquiry into whether there should be a selective 'hiving off' of departmental functions. By accountable management Fulton meant:

> holding individuals and units responsible for performance measured as objectively as possible. Its achievement depends upon identifying or establishing accountable units within government departments – units where output can be measured against costs or other criteria, and where individuals can be held personally responsible for their performance. (Fulton Report, 1968: para. 150)

The committee reacted favourably to suggestions by witnesses that accountable management is most effectively introduced when the executive activities of government – 'especially the provision of services to the community' – are separately established outside government departments (para. 188). The committee's recommendation that there should be an inquiry into the possibility of extensively 'hiving off' such functions to executive boards or corporations drew some of its inspiration from Sweden, to which the committee had paid a brief visit:

> In Sweden central departments deal in the main with policy making; they are quite small and are predominantly staffed by younger men [sic]. The task of managing and operating policies is hived off to autonomous agencies where senior staff are mainly older men of mature experience. The system is used not only for activities of a commercial kind, but also for public services in social fields. We were much impressed by it. (para. 189)

However, the committee conceded that the agency concept is not universally regarded as a good thing; for instance the committee noted that in the United States, 'the "hiving off" principle, as evidenced in the work of the independent regulatory agencies, has attracted a good deal of criticism'.

The committee saw 'no reason to believe that the dividing line between activities for which ministers are directly responsible and those for which they are not is necessarily drawn in the right place today'. But it went on to note, as a potential area of difficulty, that: 'the creation of further autonomous bodies, and the drawing of the line between them and Central Government, would raise parliamentary and constitutional issues, especially if they affected the answerability for sensitive matters such as the social and educational services' (para. 190).

Some 'hiving off' exercises took place in the 1970s – notably of the Civil Aviation Authority (1971), the Procurement Executive (1971), the Property Services Agency (1972) and the Manpower Services Commission (1974). But these bodies remained under ministerial control, rather than being managed, as Fulton had envisaged, by autonomous boards. In 1974, the Royal Ordnance Factories (privatized in the 1980s) acquired trading-fund status – enabling them to borrow money and do business on much the same lines as commercial companies, with financial targets set by ministers – and the same step was taken a year later with the Royal Mint (now a Next Steps agency). In 1977, the House of Commons Expenditure Committee expressed a view 'that hiving off is only viable in limited areas of Government and that it should be approached with caution', and it suggested that 'more attention should be devoted to developing proper control mechanisms for hived off bodies' (Expenditure Committee, 1976–7: para. 91).

Despite the fact that the Fulton Report of 1968 considered the Swedish system and suggested that lessons should be taken from it, this proposal was not taken up by government. The Next Steps Report made no mention of the Swedish experience, or indeed of important developments in New Zealand that were unfolding at the same time that the report was produced. In important respects, the Next Steps initiative differs from both these two models, and it is illuminating to compare and contrast these different approaches to the same sort of solution to the same sort of problem in three countries with different political and legal traditions.

Questions of accountability of agencies are of central importance in the United Kingdom, Sweden and New Zealand. Arrangements for accountability are made against backgrounds of different constitutional theories. In the following accounts of agency arrangements in Sweden and New Zealand, we take note of these theories and how they have influenced accountability for the agencies.

EXECUTIVE AGENCIES IN SWEDEN: LESSONS FOR THE UK?

Sweden is a constitutional monarchy, governed by a twenty-one-member Council of Ministers (Cabinet) which is *collectively* answerable to the unicameral Riksdag. There is no counterpart of the British constitutional doctrine of *individual* ministerial responsibility for the conduct of administration. Only in a few specific areas do individual ministers have specific responsibilities – for instance, that of the Minister for Foreign Affairs for Swedish embassies and consulates abroad – though ministers do have the authority to regulate the general conduct of business in their departments. This underlies the most distinctive feature of Swedish public administration, that:

> The Swedish administrative system is decentralised to a
> remarkable degree, and a great deal of routine work is hived off
> from departments to a whole host of administrative agencies
> which are legally independent of any outside authority in
> respect of day to day business. (Elder, 1970: 45)

This was the system that attracted the Fulton Committee (above). But there are differences between Sweden and Britain and the arrangements between the two countries, and the Fulton recommendations and the Next Steps arrangements do not reflect the full picture in Sweden. The Swedish agencies are headed by a director general and a board, whose membership is laid down by statute and generally includes representatives from the political parties, civil servants other than those employed in the agency in question, and trade union and employers' associations. Some agencies also have advisory councils of lay people. The regulations and general frameworks within which agencies operate are laid down by the Riksdag, and within that framework ministers may lay down policy. Government policy is formulated in Sweden against a process of extensive consultation and search for consensus (McDonald, 1992a: 10–14; 1992b: 107–9). Ministers have no power to intervene in decisions about individuals taken within agencies or to over-ride the framework laid down by the Parliament.

The absence of individual ministerial responsibility and the extensive devolution of administrative functions to independent boards explains why Swedish central departments are very small (see McDonald, 1992a: 3). It also explains the importance of extra-parliamentary forms of accountability, via a well-developed system of administrative law, including administrative courts which provide redress by way of compensation for individuals, often after the ombudsman has reported, and a powerful parliamentary ombudsman (see above).

In Sweden, as elsewhere, the distinction between policy and operational/administrative matters is far from clear and absolute, but the agency–department relationship is defined clearly in law (not the case in Britain) and is not confused by outmoded doctrines of ministerial responsibility. Agencies are accountable to Parliament and to the Cabinet as a whole, not to ministers. Ministers are not individually accountable to Parliament for the performance of agencies. Accountability of agencies is the province of the government's Chancellor of Justice (see above), the Riksdag's ombudsmen and administrative law. And freedom of information also plays a crucial part (McDonald, 1992a; 1992b).

There is a developed system or set of systems of independent 'audit' in Sweden (Richardson, 1982). The Swedish National Audit Bureau is an approximate equivalent to the British NAO, very much concerned with effectiveness auditing. The Swedish National Agency for Administrative Development is also concerned with increasing efficiency and effectiveness, and disseminates good administrative practice in organizational arrangements, programme budgeting, administrative methods, and personnel matters. In addition there is parliamentary audit, concerned for the most part with effectiveness rather than financial audit.

Sweden has long been characterized as an archetypal welfare state, with generous state support arrangements funded by high taxation. From 1932 until 1991, the Social Democrats held office (sometimes in coalition with other left-of-centre parties). Towards the end of this period, the Social Democrats had launched, in response to problems of rising unemployment, relatively high inflation and an adverse balance of trade, a 'renewal' programme, based on free market ideas, with cuts in public spending (though the welfare state was largely protected) and taxation.

The early phase of the public sector renewal programme in Sweden had a different emphasis from that of the FMI and the Next Steps:

> to achieve a wider democracy, greater freedom of choice,
> efficiency and quality, less stifling bureaucracy and, above all, to
> improve the quality of service to the public. Decentralisation,
> delegation, participation were the watchwords. (McDonald,
> 1992a: 1–2)

However, there has since been a measure of greater convergence: in Britain, there was the new populist policy-cum-rhetoric of the Citizen's Charter; in Sweden, the Social Democrats began to place greater emphasis on financial efficiency.

And the era of one-party domination in Sweden came to an abrupt halt in autumn 1991, when the government was taken over by a Conservative-led coalition, under prime minister Carl Bildt. Building upon its predecessors' conversion to free market thinking, they launched a further programme of cuts in public bureaucracy, privatization, compulsory competitive tendering, emphasis on enhanced consumer choice, performance-related pay, and the introduction of quasi-markets (OECD, 1994: 64–7).

AGENCIES IN NEW ZEALAND: MORE LESSONS FOR THE UK?

Because of New Zealand's Westminster-style constitution, public sector reform in that country has attracted particular interest in the UK. As is the case in Sweden, the process of reform, which began with the election of a Labour government in 1984, has been driven by economic and fiscal crisis. The reform process has gone through several stages: in particular, the New Zealand Civil Service was reformed under the State Sector Act 1988 (New Zealand) along lines similar in some respects to the UK Next Steps initiative, dividing much of the Civil – or public – Service into agencies. But, as is the case with Sweden, the differences are instructive.

As in the UK, the New Zealand reforms have been influenced by public choice theory, and a need to produce greater cost efficiency in the public service. The tools employed have been the injection of private sector management techniques, increased accountability and transparency (a Freedom of Information Act was introduced in 1982 and extended in 1987), the separation of politicians from managers, and clearer delineation of the roles of each. Policy decisions, and the setting and reviewing of broad objectives and 'outcomes', are the business of ministers; the delivery of outputs and operational management are the job of the chief executive. As in the UK, this separation is not easy to achieve.

Unlike the Civil Service in the UK, the public service in New Zealand has been on a statutory basis for many years. The State Sector Act 1988 and the Public Finance Act 1989 were therefore building on this formal statutory structure and meeting some of the perceived shortcomings in the way it had operated previously. The reforms were radical and based on a coherent theory about the relationship of the public service with government and Parliament. The package of reforming measures extended beyond reform of the Civil Service and finance into the field of privatization and reform of local government and the health service. We are concerned here principally with the reforms of the central public service.

The New Zealand government was conscious of the fact that the reforms affected the broader political and constitutional framework and sought to give coherence to the package in this respect: in this they were influenced to a great extent by the work of the Labour prime minister Palmer before he came to office, when he was an academic, in *Unbridled Power* (1987). But the Treasury Report 'Government Management: Brief to the Incoming Government'(1987) was an influential blueprint that was followed to a considerable extent.

The report started from basics with a 'theory of the state' which saw the role of the state as being very much linked with the effective operation of markets. As far as management of the public sector was concerned, the report stated that a government required clear objectives as well as a clear understanding of the nature and effects of its policy instruments and its limitations. Information and accountability were vital. It was the need to enhance accountability that pointed to the device of 'decoupling' performance from policy, of making clear that 'outcomes' were the business of ministers and 'outputs' the business of professional managers. These objectives were to be achieved through a series of reforms, of which the most important for our purposes are the State Sector Act 1988 and the Public Finance Act 1989.

The objectives of the State Sector Act 1988 were made explicit in the short title, as follows:

(a) To ensure that employees in the State services are imbued with the spirit of service to the community;
(b) To promote efficiency in the State services;
(c) To ensure the responsible management of the State services;
(d) To maintain appropriate standards of integrity and conduct among employees in the State services;
(e) To ensure that every employer in the State services is a good employer;
(f) To promote equal employment opportunities in the State services;
(g) To provide for the negotiation of conditions of employment in the State services.

These objectives were to be achieved by the already established State Services Commission. This body is responsible to the minister for the administration of the Act, except in matters relating to decisions on individual employees, where the commission is to act independently. The commission reports to the minister on its operations each year, and the minister must lay a copy of the report before the House of Representatives, so reporting to Parliament is indirect. The principle of ministerial responsibility is in terms expressly preserved in these reforms, although how it will work in practice is not yet clear.

The principal functions of the State Services Commission are:

● to keep the machinery of government under review;

127

- to review the efficiency, effectiveness and economy of each department, including the discharge by chief executives of their functions;
- to negotiate conditions of employment in the Public Service;
- to promote equal employment opportunities policies, personnel policies and standards of personnel administration;
- to advise on training, career development, management systems and the like.

Among its achievements is the production of a code of conduct covering the relations between ministers and civil servants in 1990. The commission resembles in many respects the British Civil Service Commissioners, but with important additional functions and clearly defined statutory objectives, powers and responsibilities.

The commission is no longer the employer of most public servants, with the exception of chief executives. The commission assists in the negotiation of the chief executives' contracts, and also reviews their annual performance agreements. Other public servants are appointed by the chief executives. The commissioners have considerable security of tenure under the Act, being removable only by the governor-general and then only for misbehaviour or incompetence; removal cannot take effect unless the House of Representatives so resolves.

The public service, for which the commission is responsible, comprises scheduled 'departments', the New Zealand equivalent of British 'agencies'. The functions of policy advice and consideration, which are still the responsibility of departments headed by ministers with permanent secretaries in charge, are carried out in New Zealand by new, small ministries separate from the large executive agency ministries, but having the status of 'agencies' headed by chief executives, thus sharpening the separation between policy and administration in a way not contemplated in the UK. So the agency concept in New Zealand covers most of the activities of the government, including many that are highly political and not, as in Britain, mainly service deliverers. They include the Audit Department, the Cabinet Office, the Crown Law Office, the Ministry of Defence (excluding the Armed Forces), the Ministry of Foreign Affairs, the Department of Justice, the Prime Minister's Office and the Treasury, to mention those that are most political. They are regarded as providing services to the government.

Each department has as its administrative head a chief executive who is responsible to the appropriate minister for carrying out the functions and duties of the department, advising the minister, the general conduct of the department, and the efficient, effective and economical management of its activities. This official is in many respects the equivalent of the permanent secretary, but with additional statutorily recognized powers and duties. He or she is accountable to the House of Representatives for his or her work, including outputs, and ministers remain accountable for policy and outcomes.

Because each department has a chief executive who operates under a contract with the minister, there is a presumption in the New Zealand reforms in favour of the work of government being discharged through executive agencies headed by chief executives. The reforms do not have the distinction found in the British model between the permanent secretary and chief executives of agencies, the latter operating generally under the permanent secretary. The New Zealand approach then is quite different from the *ad hoc*, case-by-case process of identifying those parts of the work of government in the UK that could be transferred to agencies.

But the separation of policy and administration has implications for the tradition of 'general statecraft', to borrow an expression from Wistrich (1992). The New Zealand public service has no administrative class; chief executives recruit most public servants independently. The commission and chief executives are under a duty to provide and maintain for the public service a group of senior executives with management ability, who 'shall constitute a unifying force at the most senior levels of the Public Service' (*ibid.*), and comprise the senior executive service of the public service. Wistrich comments that the trend will be for expertise to develop within sector areas, but that 'the idea of general statecraft which has been an integral part of the British Civil Service will have less chance to form' (*ibid.*: 125).

It is also significant that the reforms in New Zealand extend to some highly political or politically sensitive activities, whereas these are retained within departments in the UK, under the permanent secretary. The chief executive's position is far more explicit in the New Zealand system than in the UK. The minister may from time to time delegate to the chief executive of a department all or any of the minister's functions and powers so that, theoretically at least, a very wide range of functions even in some fairly sensitive departments could be delegated to chief executives. In exercising delegated powers or functions, the chief executive does so 'with the same effect as if they had been conferred on the chief executive directly by this section and not by delegation' (New Zealand State Sector Act 1988, Section 28(5)). The effect of this provision is to put the decision in *Carltona* v *Commissioner of Works* [1943] 2 All ER 560 on a formal statutory footing, and it mirrors in many respects the British Civil Service (Management Functions) Act 1992 (see Chapter 5).

However, delegation cannot affect or prevent the exercise of the function or power by the appropriate minister, and delegation does not affect the responsibility of the minister for the actions of a person acting under delegation. Thus, the convention of individual ministerial responsibility is expressly preserved by statute, whereas in the UK it rests on the common law and internal arrangements set out in documents such as the Armstrong Memorandum (see Appendix 1) and the Osmotherly Rules. But as in the UK, ministerial responsibility, even explicitly preserved, is not a simple doctrine to operate in New Zealand.

The chief executives are appointed by the commission after consulting the minister, and subject to acceptance of a recommendation by the governor-general; if the governor-general does not accept the commission's recommendation, he or she may direct the commission to appoint a named person. The Act sets out the criteria for appointments, which reflect the objectives of the Act set out in the short title quoted above. Vacancies should be advertised in such a manner as to enable suitable qualified persons to apply. Appointments of chief executives are for five years, renewable (the chief executives of most UK Next Steps agencies have similar tenure). Previously, tenure had been more or less permanent.

The chief executive may delegate any of his or her powers or functions to an employee or a member of the senior executive service, with the written consent of the minister if the function is one delegated to the chief executive by the minister. Delegation does not, however, prevent the exercise of any function or power by the chief executive, nor does it affect the responsibility of the chief executive for the actions of any person acting under the delegation.

Chief executives make all appointments in the senior executive service in the department, on merit. Appointments to the senior executive service are for five years, renewable, with provisions for removal 'for just cause or excuse' (New Zealand State Sector Act 1988, Section 53). Chief executives also appoint (and remove) other employees, on merit.

Finally, 'Every person commits an offence against this section who directly or indirectly solicits or endeavours to influence the Commission or any Commissioner or any chief executive' (*ibid.*, Section 85(1)), although this does not apply to any person giving information or advice or making representations.

As indicated earlier, the State Sector Act was only one of a pair of statutes reforming the public service: the other was the Public Finance Act 1989. This aimed to link the appropriation of funds provided by Parliament to performance. The reforms focus on the interests of the government in 'purchasing' outputs from the public service, and in the efficient use of publicly owned assets. Departments have to supply information and meet certain standards of proof of performance. Transparency and accountability are central: a duty to report on performance is imposed on departments, by way of monthly reports to the minister, with a copy to the Minister of Finance, giving the financial position and cash flow for the department. Some departments whose outputs are not 'contestable', such as the policy-making departments, are subject to 'accrual accounting'; others, including the service-delivery departments, are subject to a more commercial form of accounting. The Act focuses on departmental outputs, and this makes for greater clarity about the objectives of the department, which in turn improves the sense of direction and priority of the department – as well as facilitating accountability.

COMMENT AND COMPARISONS

In sharp contrast with Sweden and New Zealand, the British Constitution remains blighted by the widening gap between the *theory* of individual ministerial responsibility and its *practice*. In an age of big government (still big, despite the cutbacks of the 1980s and 1990s), it is simply not credible to pretend that ministers can be answerable for all the actions and inactions of their officials, and for every last detail of departmental business. Yet ministers and civil servants have found it convenient to maintain the fiction that this is the case, in the face of what they, along with everyone else, know to be a very different reality.

Despite Fulton's interest in the Swedish system, and the superficial similarities between the agency system in Britain and the Swedish model, there are in fact some very significant differences. Next Steps was an evolutionary development from the FMI, launched in 1982, the rationale of which was to improve the efficiency of financial management and achieve better value for money in central government by devolving budgetary responsibilities. The implicit purpose of Next Steps was to make the FMI work better. One important by-product has been a loosening of the Treasury's grip on day-to-day financial management. Having partially freed the management of agencies from central control, though they are responsible for meeting the targets set out in framework agreements negotiated with the centre, the Citizen's Charter makes agencies and their chief executives more directly accountable to newly empowered consumer-citizens.

The Swedish system of administrative boards is a mature system, embedded in a different political culture (including a resilient and expensive welfare support system and an expectation of much greater openness in government) and a very different constitutional-legal tradition from those of the UK. Being a mature system (albeit one that has recently being undergoing major changes), it has grappled with issues that have caused some concern in the British context – for instance, coherent career planning in an increasingly fragmented Civil Service: Oonagh McDonald suggests that something along the lines of the Swedish National Agency for Administrative Development might be a useful model to adopt in the context of the Next Steps programme (McDonald, 1992a: 23). It should also be acknowledged that coherent central management of a devolved system may be much easier to achieve in a smaller country with a more compact public sector.

The biggest differences between the United Kingdom and Sweden are the constitutional-legal ones. The process of reform in the UK has been hampered by the incubus of individual ministerial responsibility, which forms no part of the Swedish constitutional tradition. 'Alternative' forms of accountability, such as ombudsmen and judicial review, have begun to attain greater prominence in the UK, but they are still considered secondary to parliamentary accountability. In Sweden, public administration and administrative reform are founded on public law. Accountability to courts, tribunals and ombudsmen is integral to the devolved responsibilities of administrative boards and local authorities. Change is underpinned by legislation and debated with reference to legal and constitutional, as well as political and social, implications. It is in this area that UK reformers have most to learn from their Swedish counterparts – and indeed from those in other European countries.

The New Zealand model of reform has been much more radical than the Next Steps programme in the UK, in particular in its use of policy contracts. Patricia Greer describes this as 'an extreme solution' (Greer, 1994: 115) to the dilemma of how to separate policy and operational issues. The minister is responsible for policy decisions, for which he or she answers to Parliament. The minister is also responsible for purchasing all the services required for the department, from departmental agencies. The latter operate as business units and are required to have business plans. Units responsible for 'output delivery' (for instance, provision of income support) in turn buy the support services they need, either from support agencies attached to the department or from outside the department altogether. The heads of agencies are accountable to Parliament for the day-to-day operation of their businesses, and those in senior policy roles are also responsible for the quality and timeliness of the advice they give to ministers.

This model was lauded by some of the witnesses giving evidence to the TCSC in its 1992–4 inquiry into the UK Civil Service. In particular, Graham Mather, President of the European Policy Forum, advocated the introduction of departmental policy directorates, along with fixed-term contracts for the top three Civil Service grades: he suggested the introduction of policy contracts along New Zealand lines as a remedy for what he called a 'loop of policy failure' (TCSC, 1993: Q. 282). There are no signs, as yet, of a movement in Britain towards such a radical solution. Indeed, the momentum of administrative change in New Zealand slowed down somewhat in the early 1990s.

Once again, as with Sweden, the most marked contrast with the UK has been the extent to which change has been discussed in constitutional terms, and implemented through the medium of statute law. Next Steps and the Citizen's Charter, as we have noted, have made only the faintest impression on the statute book.

The constitutional theories, political traditions, population sizes and geography of New Zealand, Sweden and the United Kingdom are different in many respects, and this has to be borne in mind when making comparisons. Nevertheless, considerations of the arrangements in other countries can give us insights into our own, and enable us to imagine how things might be done differently – and better. In particular, administrative law, in the sense of a set of statutorily backed arrangements for establishing and controlling public administration, should be considered as an instrument that might make up for the weaknesses of ministerial accountability in securing effective redress of grievances and effective performance. Techniques such as enforceable duties of disclosure and rights of access to information, direct citizen access to a strong ombudsman with powers to deal with questions of illegality as well as maladministration, the definition of the duties of civil servants and agencies and their relationships with ministers, and requirements for direct reporting by agencies to Parliament could enhance the British arrangements.

9

Accountability and the Public Service: Towards a New Administrative Law

In this final chapter we review the findings in our earlier discussions and draw together some threads in the issues of responsibility and accountability raised by the public service reforms on which we have been focusing, particularly the executive agency initiative and the Citizen's Charter arrangements. We consider how appropriate and effective current arrangements for accountability and responsibility are, and what directions might be taken in seeking to enhance them where necessary.

A sharper distinction is evolving between *accountability* – the duty to explain or justify and then the duty to make amends to anyone who has suffered loss or injustice if something has gone wrong – and *responsibility* – having a job to do, and being liable to take the blame when things go wrong. In the British system, accountability for public services is broadly reserved to ministers. The latter may have to bear responsibility as well: for instance if their policy is found to have been defective, or if an agency within a department was not properly established, funded and staffed (as with the Child Support Agency) or, perhaps, if ministerial interference in the day-to-day operational running of an agency were to make it impossible for the Chief Executive to do his or her job properly (as may have been the case with the Prison Service). But in practice (particularly in an agency context) civil servants often have to carry all or part of the responsibility.

Some observers, particularly the more cynical ones, may argue that there is nothing very novel about this and that it has long been the case that ministers are only too happy to take responsibility, as well as being accountable, for successes, but are quick to attribute any blame to their officials. But the gap between theory and practice has been widened by the development of the Next Steps programme. When that programme

134

was launched, in 1988, it was explicitly stated that the conventions of ministerial responsibility would remain in place; and, according to those conventions, ministers have the exclusive right to explain and justify what has happened in their departments, and officials have no right – or duty – to do so without authority. Hence the effectiveness of both accountability and responsibility are undermined in the British system.

It is this weakness that has produced calls for officials to be directly accountable to select committees of the House of Commons, and for the development of alternative mechanisms of accountability such as the use of charters (which expose public servants to pressures from 'empowered' citizen-consumers), tribunals and the courts (providing various kinds of legal redress), and the PCA (who can hold officials to account for maladministration).

Three aspects of mechanisms of accountability and responsibility are important:

- The release of information, whether through a duty to explain and justify or through public rights of access to relevant information. The British arrangements for officials' responsibility prevents them from unauthorized disclosure and does not impose on them any positive duty to disclose.
- The existence and clarity of criteria for evaluating conduct. These are lacking, for instance, in relation to the accountability of ministers to Parliament.
- The availability of sanctions or remedies if fault is found.

The British arrangements, again, are ambivalent, since the person in control, the minister, will not be liable to punishment if things have gone wrong, only to a weak and unpredictable political duty to make amends.

The reforms of public services over the last decade or more, described in earlier chapters, have involved the development of techniques which might be called – borrowing the title of Osborne and Gaebler's bestseller (1992) – 'reinventing government'. The aims have been to increase the efficiency and effectiveness of services, and to obtain better value for money in their delivery.

Techniques have included enhancing the position of the 'consumer' of services, encouraging competition rather then monopoly, and adopting or adapting market mechanisms. The Citizen's Charter sets out the criteria against which the standards of services to individuals are to be measured, and provides complaints procedures, but does not provide legal rights or legal avenues to pursue complaints – illustrating the preference in the British tradition for non-legal arrangements in public services. Government by contract also provides the criteria for auditing performance, and here there are legally enforceable contractual remedies available in some instances between state bodies and the providers with which they contract; but not generally for the 'consumer' of the service in question.

Depoliticization brings out the need for non-political accountability mechanisms – redress of grievance opportunities through the Citizen's Charter or access to the ombudsmen, for instance. Institutional reforms, notably the executive agency arrangements, in some ways enhance the accountability of chief executives to ministers and Parliament, and to the interested member of the public, since criteria are developed in framework documents, performance agreements and corporate plans which enable performance to be measured. But these arrangements distance the agencies from Parliament when individual grievances are raised, suggesting a need to enhance other mechanisms by, for instance, requiring the release of more information to the public or giving those with grievances direct access to ombudsmen. Parliament also has had no role in the design of the executive agency arrangements, since they have been put in place under the power of the government to organize and reorganize the Civil Service under the Civil Service Order in Council, in which Parliament has no say.

In sum, public service reforms in the United Kingdom have increased the *responsibilities* of managers of public services – the extent to which they personally have identifiable jobs to do, and for which they will take blame if things go wrong. But this process, we suggest, has not put in place adequate mechanisms of *accountability* – the duty either of managers or ministers to answer questions, provide information and make amends – for these responsibilities. It has been maintained that ministers remain, in accordance with nineteenth-century constitutional theory, responsible to Parliament for policy and have duties to put right what has gone wrong in departments and agencies within departments, but without taking 'responsibility' for it in the sense of accepting blame. Managers themselves are not, supposedly, accountable except to ministers and, under the Citizen's Charter, to aggrieved individuals; and in particular they are not, according to tradition, accountable to Parliament other than in the important but narrow context of their appearances before the PAC, as financial accounting officers. In practice, however, chief executives of Next Steps agencies appearing before select committees are liable to find themselves personally exposed to questioning, criticism and pressure of a very direct kind, as the experience of the Chief Executive of the Employment Service before the Select Committee for the PCA indicates (Chapter 7).

For the most part, the changes that have been taking place in public services are not unique to the United Kingdom but have been introduced also, in a variety of versions, in other advanced Western democracies. We have focused on Sweden, where many of the arrangements now being adopted in the United Kingdom have been operating, Swedish style, for many years; and on New Zealand, which has trodden a path across the landscape very similar in many respects to that being followed in the UK, with which it shares a 'Westminister' constitution. Both of those countries, however, have mapped out their agency arrangements and redress of grievance mechanisms much more explicitly and in legal terms, on roads and motorways rather than the unsignposted tracks that criss-cross the British Constitution, and against a hinterland of well-articulated constitutional theory. Unlike the United Kingdom, New Zealand and Sweden have in place statutory rights of access to official information, criteria for 'audit' of public service provision, strong and accessible ombudsmen, sanctions, and remedies for grievances – in other words, a strong system of administrative law.

Traditionally, the method of seeking to 'control' the Civil Service in the UK has been to regulate *procedures* both for recruitment and promotion in the service and for actual decision making, with requirements for neutrality and impartiality, fairness and natural justice, satisfaction of legitimate expectations, the following of guidelines and so on. These requirements are found in a range of sources, such as the Civil Service Order in Council, and decisions of the courts on applications for judicial review (see Chapter 5). Relatively little attention has been paid until the last twenty years or so to the outputs and outcomes of policy. The Next Steps programme and the Citizen's Charter mark an important shift of emphasis in this direction.

This shift has produced expressions of concern that the older and valuable traditions of the public service may be sacrificed to efficiency, effectiveness and market forces. The intention of the initiatives, however, is to have the best of both worlds, preserving the 'glue' that holds the Civil Service together – traditions of professional public service, neutrality, fairness and the like – at the same time as increasing efficiency and effectiveness. The shift in emphasis from inputs to outcomes may have implications for judicial review and the content of the law, which have hitherto matched the traditional ethos and tradition of government and the Civil Service by focusing on decision-making and policy-making *processes* rather than 'merits' or outcome.

A number of underlying themes and theories have influenced public service reform. A strong influence has been the desire to improve the Three Es of efficiency, effectiveness and economy in government, for both ideological and economic reasons. This set of considerations goes back well before the advent of the Thatcher administration in 1979, but attention focused on it more sharply under Thatcher's premiership. To be added to this is a further 'E', namely the empowerment of the individual 'consumer' of public service, which is a much newer feature of the landscape, becoming visible in the early 1980s with the granting of security of tenure to council tenants and the right to buy a council home. It then spread to increased parental choice of schools, the possibility of schools opting out of local authority control, and since 1991 the Citizen's Charter initiative and the promulgation of special charters for specific classes of consumer – jobseekers, patients and so on.

The techniques adopted by government to promote these four Es have been influenced by New Public Management theories, which assume that the public sector has much to learn from the private sector, and lead inevitably to the promotion of a contractual, corporatized set of relationships between government and agencies providing services on its behalf, in place of the dominant administrative paradigm of the post-Northcote Trevelyan reforms.

The four Es also lead logically to raising – or, perhaps more appropriately, modifying – the status of the recipient of public services from that of *passive* passenger, patient, claimant or citizen, who can use the political process to 'voice' complaints, to the *active* position of choosy and well-informed customer or client. For the most part, however, this newly empowered citizen is not a customer or client with legal rights but one with rights to complain, whose traditional access to the political system for resolution of grievances has been reduced by the reforms – the effect of which has been to direct complaints to the service provider and away from ministers.

Public choice theory has also been influential in public service reform. The aspects of the theory that have been taken on board are the assumption that public servants are, given the chance, self-serving 'log-rollers' and 'utility maximizers', who will be primarily concerned to promote their own interests rather than those of the government or the public they are supposed to serve. In the early 1980s, local authority councillors and public service trade unions were seen as focuses for this set of attitudes across the public sector.

This aspect of public choice theory accounts for much of the reform and change in local government (compulsory competitive tendering, corporatization in schools, and consumerization), and the trade union reform programme that was implemented in the 1980s. It is also influential in the strategy introduced in 1994 of giving civil servants in the most responsible positions individual contracts and performance-related pay, and of permitting chief executives of agencies the right to recruit and to fix pay rates and terms and conditions of service with those they employ. A side effect of this arrangement has been to weaken further Civil Service trade unions, as well as to introduce incentives and disincentives more prominently into the employment contracts of public servants. The consequent fragmentation and individualization of the Civil Service has raised questions about how the public service ethos can be preserved.

Public choice theory has also been a factor in the introduction of the Citizen's Charter, one purpose of which is to enhance the position of the individual consumer of public services in relations with public servants, by giving the individual 'rights' – though not legally enforceable 'rights' for the most part – to complain and to receive a certain level of service from those with whom he or she has dealings in the service.

The last of the 'themes and theories' we have identified as being influential in public service reform has been the search for the 'irreducible/inescapable' core of government, and the desire on the part of government to ask not 'What can we sell?'(which was the question in the privatization period), but 'What must we keep?' – the implication being that other activities can be sold off, contracted out, or abandoned altogether by government.

PUBLIC MANAGEMENT AND MARKETS: THE LEGAL IMPLICATIONS

As we have seen, the period with which we are concerned has seen a transition from 'public administration' to 'public management' and a hostility to 'bureaucracy' or 'bureaucratism'. In particular, there has been a shift of focus away from inputs, procedures and outputs (the traditional concerns of Weberian bureaucracies) and towards outcomes, which are of greater importance in the private sector. There has also been a shift towards emphasizing the responsibility of the individual and recognizing the limited capacity of the state to provide for the needs of all effectively, even if that were something the state wished to do, which under a Conservative government it was not.

The realization of the limitations on the state's ability to run things has led to a preference for leaving matters to market forces, either genuine ones or artificially created ones, and of course it is central to a market system that there should be a developed system of (enforceable) contract law. Hayek and Friedman were very influential in this set of developments. Reliance on the market in principle would suggest depoliticization of activity, and this has been seen in many reforms in the public service; but the market relies, for its effective operation and the avoidance of monopoly and monopolistic abuses, on a strong, centralized regulatory function. Hence the seeming paradox between the free market-based economy and the strong state identified by Gamble (1994) as explaining the combination of market strategy and the considerable centralization that resulted from government policies in the 1980s.

This reference to the importance of contract and thus of legal personality in the form of corporate existence in public service reform leads us to the legal, or more appropriately non-legal, aspects of public administration generally and of the reforms with which we have been concerned in particular. Two strong traditions in British government have been to rely on mechanisms of political rather than legal accountability to secure high standards of public administration, and to deal with perceived needs for improvement administratively and incrementally, adding procedures and institutions to the existing infrastructure as and when pressures become irresistible, rather than legally and as part of a coherent vision or framework for public administration in a democracy. Reform has tended to be driven by tactics rather than by longer-term strategic considerations.

Unlike the position in New Zealand, there is no statute or formal code that establishes and governs public administration in the United Kingdom, and what law there is on the subject is to be found only partly in statutes and case law, and largely in subordinate legislation, notably the Civil Service Order in Council. That is not to say that there are no norms or criteria for measuring performance in the public service, only that they are not justiciable. Many of the procedures and processes of public administration are not governed by law in the conventional sense at all, but increasingly by codes of practice, notes of guidance, the Citizen's Charter, framework documents, and unwritten rules passed on from one generation of public administrators to the next by a process akin to osmosis. But these written and unwritten rules are crucial to the operation of the service and its accountability, and their proliferation in recent years can be seen as part of a growing process of normativization of the public service, which represents a tacit acknowledgement of the limitations of ministerial accountability that is not fleshed out by statements of what is to be expected of public administrators.

It is the clarity of criteria that commonly separates legal and often administrative accountability from public or political accountability. In judicial review, for example, the criteria against which decisions and actions are measured (legality, procedural propriety and 'irrationality') are in principle limited in number and fixed (although they are not as clear as many would like them to be), and the procedures of the courts are supposed to secure that questions are determined according to these limited criteria. By contrast there is, as the Nolan Committee on standards in public life found, very little in the way of explicit criteria against which to judge the performance and conduct of ministers or MPs.

Procedures are crucial to the effectiveness of accountability. The procedures of the courts have many advantages over, for instance, those

of the Houses of Parliament (behind which lie the ultimate accountability of politicians to the perils of the ballot box), notably openness,
predictability, and protection of the individual. But often they will not
be suited to the task of imposing accountability on government,
especially because of their adversarial nature, and the legitimacy of
judicial intervention in areas to do with politics and government may be
open to doubt because of the administrative inexperience and non-
accountability of the judges themselves. Other, legally based institutions, such as auditors, inquiries or the PCA (see below), may well adopt
more effective procedures than the courts and more appropriate criteria
than those used in the Houses of Parliament.

The PCA is a form of bureaucratic auditor. He or she applies the
'maladministration' criteria, elaborated in the 'Crossman catalogue' at
the second reading of the Parliamentary Commissioner Bill in 1966
('bias, neglect, inattention, delay, incompetence, inaptitude, perversity,
turpitude, arbitrariness and so on') and in successive reports over the
years. These, though general, are firmer than the criteria of ministerial
responsibility. The PCA's procedures enable investigators to have access
to files and to interview witnesses so that the report can be an informed
one.

Similarly, the Comptroller and Auditor General and the NAO
operate 'financial audit' processes according to set criteria to do with
financial regularity, propriety and value for money. These procedures,
too, are more likely to produce informed assessments of government –
and other – actions than either ministerial responsibility or judicial
review could do.

There is then an important and developing role for various forms of
audit in the British system, as there has been for many years in Sweden.
But Power's warning (1994) that audit as a mechanism for accountability can substitute quantitative for qualitative measuring and undermine trust in the public service needs to be heeded. It would be wrong
to assume that audit can ever substitute for more qualitative forms of
accountability.

This brings us to the question of sanctions and accountability. In
judicial review and statutory appeals (planning appeals, for example)
the sanctions are potentially coercive (*M. v Home Office*; see Chapter 5),
although they will sometimes be discretionary. By comparison, the
conventions of ministerial responsibility, partly but not entirely because
they provide only very fluid criteria for the assessment of ministerial
performance, are not backed up by coercion. Rarely will ministers resign
because of failures of public administration; almost never will they
personally make amends to individuals, though they may require their
departments to do so.

But not all mechanisms of accountability entail, nor need they entail, resort to coercion as a sanction, if other mechanisms are effective in practice. In Sweden, for example, the freedom of information regime and the ombudsman provide effective mechanisms of accountability without the need for recourse to coercive measures (McDonald, 1992a, 1992b; Lundvik, 1983b). In the United Kingdom, the findings and reports of the Comptroller and Auditor General and the NAO are effectively binding (many of them could be coercively enforced). The recommendations of the PCA are not formally binding, though in practice the political sanctions ensure compliance. (The recommendations of the Commissioners for Local Administration are disregarded more commonly than those of the PCA, for reasons to do with the weakness of political sanctions in local government.)

THE CROWN: ONE AND INDIVISIBLE

The legal basis of public administration in central government in the United Kingdom differs greatly from those in New Zealand and Sweden. The government is 'the Crown', and a significant aspect of this is the doctrine of indivisibility. This makes it legally impossible for agencies to contract with their ministers or indeed for any parts of the Crown to contract with one another. This 'indivisibility' also buttresses the view that the Civil Service has no legal personality separate from that of the government of the day, which in turn means that civil servants are not personally directly responsible to Parliament, and ministers are accountable for everything that happens in their departments. An implication of this position is that neither ministers nor civil servants are 'responsible' to Parliament in the sense of taking the blame for administrative as opposed to policy errors. As we have seen, this doctrine operates to limit the ability of Parliament to hold civil servants accountable for what goes right or wrong in an agency; but ministerial accountability to Parliament does not serve to secure high standards of service and performance generally or to make transparent why things do go right or wrong.

This position can be contrasted with that in New Zealand, where the bulk of the public service has been separated legally from the political arm of the executive, and heads of agencies are directly accountable to ministers and Parliament. In Sweden, as we saw in Chapter 8, the chief executives of agencies are directly accountable to the Cabinet as a whole and to the Parliament, and ministers are not individually accountable to Parliament for agencies except for the policy under which they operate.

A crucial legal aspect of the Civil Service in the United Kingdom is that its organization and reorganization are carried on by government in

exercise of common law powers. There is therefore no formal requirement for Parliament to have any input into reorganization or to
appointments in the service. It is because of this legal position that the
introduction of executive agencies in the Civil Service has taken place
without any prior approval from Parliament, and its ability to scrutinize
the arrangements and affect how they work has been minimal. Here the
comparison with New Zealand is informative, for there and in Sweden
the public service is statute-based.

The trend in recent cases has been to accept that civil servants have
contracts of employment with the Crown, although under those contracts they are strictly dismissible at will. This position increases the
employment protection available to civil servants, but it represents a
shift away from the earlier tradition, which was that civil servants were
'public' servants, owing duties to a higher-order public interest, rather
than people who owed duties to the government of the day. In other
words, a side effect of the move to conceiving the relationship between
the Crown and civil servants as one of contractual employment is to
undermine the public service ethos, as enshrined in the law relating to
the relationship between the Crown and its servants (Lewis and Longley,
1994).

It is difficult to measure the effect on the public service ethos of the
recent reforms in the public sector. This issue of ethos might be
regarded as a fifth 'E' in the catalogue of themes and theories of public
service reform. In the century or so after Northcote Trevelyan, that
ethos itself evolved into the foundation for a high standard of service and
propriety in the service; but this foundation could well be undermined
if the ethos changed as a result of the introduction of such alterations as
performance-related pay, individual employment contracts, and the
actual discharge of functions by private enterprises under contract, as
with the use of security firms to run prisons or transport prisoners under
secure conditions.

Hence, as we saw in Chapter 6, the TCSC called for a new Civil
Service code. The *First Report of the Committee on Standards in Public Life*
(1995) recommended immediate introduction of this code (Chapter 3)
and the government agreed (Cm 2931, 1995) and introduced it at the
end of 1995 (see Appendix 2). The government also accepted the Nolan
Committee's recommendations about formulating standards of conduct
for ministers generally, including their relations with civil servants. The
Nolan Committee recommended too, and the government accepted, a
revision of *Questions of Procedure for Ministers* (1992), with a new section,
to be renamed 'Conduct and Procedure for Ministers', setting out the
ethical principles and rules that apply. These include, for instance, the
instruction that: 'Ministers must not use public resources for party
political purposes. They must uphold the political impartiality of the

Civil Service, and not ask civil servants to act in any other way which would conflict with the Civil Service Code' (Cm 2931, 1995: Annex A).

Although public administration is subject to the rule of law, notably in the important but limited sense that all actions that interfere with the rights and liberties of individuals must have a legal, usually statutory, basis, the ability of the courts to control public administration is restricted in a number of ways. Moreover, there is a very high degree of secrecy about government activity, based partly on statute and partly on the law relating to confidentiality and employment contracts, and reinforced by the inhibitions of civil servants that flow from the traditional rules about ministerial responsibility. This makes much of what government does impenetrable, and hence difficult to challenge in the courts, or anywhere else.

As from 1993, when the *Open Government* White Paper was introduced, the PCA investigates breaches of the code with a view to determining whether there has been maladministration resulting in injustice to an individual. But there is no *prima facie* obligation on government to disclose information. The courts have been dabbing away at this blot on the public service landscape in recent decisions, liberalizing the law relating to public interest immunity certificates and developing a duty to give reasons in many (but not all) situations. The development of various forms of audit has also eroded the rock of secrecy in government, with the Comptroller and Auditor General, the NAO and the PCA having access to files in investigating, respectively, the propriety and VFM of expenditure, and complaints of maladministration.

These points about the limits of the law in public administration raise the issue of whether administrative law will develop means of evaluating and controlling outcomes, in relation either to particular decisions affecting individuals, or even to general decisions of a more political nature. At present there are of course some mechanisms for reviewing decisions that affect individuals 'on the merits' through the tribunal system, and the ombudsmen venture to a degree into the field of merits where a thoroughly unlawful or bad decision is under investigation; but there is nothing as general as the New Zealand ombudsman's power to investigate bad decisions, or the powers of the Australian Administrative Review Tribunal, which can effectively review the merits and substitute its own decision on a matter.

New Zealand and Australia, both offspring of the common law approach, and civil law systems through councils of state (the French Conseil d'Etat and the Italian Consiglio di Stato, for example) permit substantive review. Given this, it is open to consideration whether the shift within public administration to holding bodies politically, publicly and administratively accountable for results, outcomes and outputs should be, or will be, reflected in the range of arrangements for legal accountability, whether to ombudsmen, courts or tribunals of various kinds. The logic of the current reforms would seem to point in the direction of such a development.

An extension of the jurisdiction of the PCA to embrace illegality, as in Sweden and New Zealand for example, could help to counter the problems experienced by the high court in dealing with applications for judicial review, since these have increased in number enormously over the last decade or so, and are both expensive to deal with and slow. It would not be appropriate for individuals to be *required* to seek to refer complaints of illegality to the PCA before they could apply for judicial review, and the findings of the PCA should not be binding. But, subject to those safeguards, extension of the PCA's powers into the field of illegality could greatly enhance the effectiveness of provisions for redress of grievance. The PCA could also be given an explicit role in developing 'best practice' guidance, and hence have a substantial and recognized input into improving the quality of administration, as well as providing redress after the event. It would also make good sense to remove the present bar, not found in other ombudsman systems, upon his or her investigating complaints about personnel-related grievances in the Civil Service.

The use of complaints adjudicators in some services (see Chapter 3) seems to have been a success, and consideration should be given to extending this sort of appointment. These adjudicators supplement the PCA channel, but MPs are not involved in referring complaints to them. It is likely that, if further such appointments are made, the role of MPs in the redress of grievances will become less significant, and their energies may be directed more into the field of the general quality of administration and government policy. Whether MPs themselves would welcome such a shift is a moot point.

A number of other important issues arise: should the United Kingdom Civil Service be placed on a statutory basis, as it has been for many years in New Zealand, so that contractualization and corporatization can be legally enforced, and provisions could be made for the judicial scrutiny of framework documents? This has been resisted on the grounds that it would allegedly lead to greater inflexibility in the management of the Civil Service, and encourage the use of litigation to sort out problems in the public service. In so far as 'inflexibility' appears to be a euphemism for 'management on the basis of clear principles and criteria', and given that occasional recourse to the courts to resolve uncertainties may well be in the public interest, these objections seem unconvincing.

Bogdanor (1994) has made a number of radical suggestions for improving the accountability of executive agencies to Parliament. He proposes that the relationship between ministers and officials needs to be made explicitly contractual, so that specific responsibilities are delegated to officials and put into statutory form in, for example, a statutory instrument. Ministers would then remain responsible only for the terms of the delegation. Thus the framework document would be converted into a legal document that would in the last resort be subject to judicial interpretation, and might put the chief executive in a stronger position to resist ministerial interference.

Second, Bogdanor proposes that chief executives of Next Steps agencies should be directly accountable to the select committees of the House of Commons. This would need to be formalized in some way, perhaps by means of a statement that the Osmotherly Rules should not apply to certain types of evidence given to select committees by the chief executives. Policy advice given by chief executives could continue to be protected. Bogdanor raises the possibility of Parliament voting to reduce the salary of a chief executive if he or she is found to be in error, thus trying to plug the sanctions gap in present arrangements by extending to civil servants a remedy that is, theoretically, available to Parliament against ministers. Despite the government's repeated reiteration of the importance of ministers, not civil servants, being accountable to Parliament, the trend in recent years has been increasingly for select committees to expect chief executives to give their own answers and receive criticism from the committees (the Employment Service case study points about the Select Committee for the PCA illustrates the point; see Chapter 7), and modifications along the lines Bogdanor proposes would be giving recognition to changing realities.

Giles Radice MP, discussing executive agencies (see Chapter 3), has remarked:

> Accountability is in its infancy, but there is a strong case for
> arguing that parliamentary accountability [of agencies] will
> need to be supplemented by a strengthened system of
> administrative justice, a more powerful ombudsman and a
> freedom of information act. (HC Deb., 1990–1: vol. 191, col.
> 687)

It is suggested that a programme of reform, including some or all of the possible changes discussed above, is urgently needed to repair some of the cracks that have appeared in the present arrangements for accountability and responsibility for the delivery and management of public services. The cumulative effects of recent public sector reform have exposed the extent and the width of those cracks, and in some cases widened them. In the absence of such reforms, the accountability gap that existed, thinly camouflaged by outmoded constitutional rhetoric, even before the New Public Management Revolution will continue to grow wider as that revolution continues.

Appendix 1 The Armstrong Memorandum

This is an abridgement of the 1987 version:

Civil servants are servants of the Crown. For all practical purposes the Crown in this context means ... the Government of the day ... The Civil Service as such has no constitutional personality or responsibility separate from the Government of the day ...

The Civil Service serves the Government of the day as a whole, that is to say Her Majesty's Ministers collectively, and the Prime Minister is Minister for the Civil Service. The duty of the individual civil servant is first and foremost to the Minister of the Crown who is in charge of the Department in which he or she is serving ...

It is the duty of civil servants to serve their Ministers with integrity and to the best of their ability. In their dealings with the public, civil servants should always bear in mind that people have a right to expect that their affairs will be dealt with sympathetically, efficiently and promptly ...

The British Civil Service is a non-political and professional career service subject to a code of rules and disciplines. Civil servants are required to serve the duly constituted Government of the day, of whatever political complexion. It is of the first importance that civil servants should conduct themselves in such a way as to deserve and retain the confidence of Ministers, and to be able to establish the same relationship with those whom they may be required to serve in some future Administration ...

... In the determination of policy the civil servant has no constitutional responsibility or role distinct from that of the

Minister. Subject to the conventions limiting the access of
Ministers to the papers of previous Administrations, it is the
duty of the civil servant to make available to the Minister all the
information and experience at his or her disposal which may have
a bearing on the policy decision . . . , and to give the Minister
honest and impartial advice, without fear or favour, and whether
the advice accords with the Minister's view or not . . .

Civil servants are under an obligation to keep the confidences
to which they become privy in the course of their work . . .

When a civil servant gives evidence to parliamentary select committees (in respect of which there is a separate memorandum of guidance,
the so-called Osmotherly Rules):

he or she does so as the representative of the Minister in charge
of the Department and subject to the Minister's instructions,
and is accountable to the Minister for the evidence which he or
she gives . . . It is not acceptable for a serving or former civil
servant to seek to frustrate policies or decisions of Ministers by
disclosure outside the Government of information to which he
or she has had access as a civil servant.

. . . In the very unlikely event of a civil servant being asked to
do something which he or she believes would put him or her in
clear breach of the law, the matter should be reported to a senior
officer or to the Principal Establishment Officer, who should if
necessary seek the advice of the Legal Adviser to the
Department. If legal advice confirms that the action would be
likely to be held to be unlawful, the matter should be reported
in writing to the Permanent Head of the Department.

If a civil servant considers that he or she is being asked:

to act in a manner which appears to him or her to be improper,
unethical or in breach of constitutional conventions, or to
involve possible maladministration, or be otherwise inconsistent
with the standards of conduct prescribed in this memorandum
and in the relevant Civil Service codes and guides . . . the matter
should be reported to a senior officer, and if appropriate to the
Permanent Head of the Department.

. . . A civil servant should not decline to take or abstain from
taking, an action because to do so would conflict with his or her
personal opinions . . . ; he or she should consider the possibility
or declining only if taking or abstaining from the action in
question is felt to be directly contrary to deeply held personal
conviction on a fundamental issue of conscience . . .

A civil servant who feels that to act or to abstain from acting in a particular way, or to acquiesce in a particular decision or course of action, would raise for him or her a fundamental issue of conscience, or is so profoundly opposed to a policy as to feel unable conscientiously to administer it in accordance with the [required] standards ... should consult a senior officer. If necessary, and if the problem cannot be resolved by any other means, the civil servant may take the matter up with the Permanent Head of the Department and also has a right, in the last resort, to have the matter referred to the Head of the Home Civil Service through the Permanent Head of the Department ... If the matter still cannot be resolved on a basis which the civil servant is able to accept, he or she must either carry out his or her instructions or resign from the public service.

Appendix 2 The Civil Service Code

1. The constitutional and practical role of the Civil Service is, with integrity, honesty, impartiality and objectivity, to assist the duly constituted Government, of whatever political complexion, in formulating policies of the Government, carrying out decisions of the Government, and in administering public services for which the Government is responsible.

2. Civil servants are servants of the Crown. Constitutionally, the Crown acts on the advice of Ministers and, subject to the provisions of this Code, civil servants owe their loyalty to the duly constituted Government.

3. This Code should be seen in the context of the duties and responsibilities of Ministers set out in Questions of Procedure for Ministers which include:
    -   accountability to Parliament;
    -   the duty to give Parliament and the public as full information as possible about the policies, decisions and actions of the Government, and not to deceive or knowingly mislead Parliament and the public;
    -   the duty not to use public resources for party political purposes, to uphold the political impartiality of the Civil Service, and not to ask civil servants to act in any way which would conflict with the Civil Service Code;
    -   the duty to give fair consideration and due weight to informed and impartial advice from civil servants, as well as to other considerations and advice, in reaching decisions; and
    -   the duty to comply with the law, including international law

    and treaty obligations, and to uphold the administration of
    justice;

together with the duty to familiarise themselves with the
contents of this Code.

4. Civil servants should serve the duly constituted Government
   in accordance with the principles set out in this Code and
   recognising:
   - the accountability of civil servants to the Minister or, as the
     case may be, the office holder in charge of their depart-
     ment;
   - the duty of all public officers to discharge public functions
     reasonably and according to the law;
   - the duty to comply with the law, including international law
     and treaty obligations, and to uphold the administration of
     justice; and
   - ethical standards governing particular professions.

5. Civil servants should conduct themselves with integrity,
   impartiality and honesty. They should give honest and
   impartial advice to Ministers, without fear or favour, and
   make all information relevant to a decision available to
   Ministers. They should not deceive or knowingly mislead
   Ministers, Parliament or the public.

6. Civil servants should endeavour to deal with the affairs of
   the public sympathetically, efficiently, promptly and
   without bias or maladministration.

7. Civil servants should endeavour to ensure the proper,
   effective and efficient use of public money.

8. Civil servants should not misuse their official position or
   information acquired in the course of their official duties to
   further their private interests or those of others. They should
   not receive benefits of any kind from a third party which
   might compromise their personal judgement or integrity.

9. Civil servants should conduct themselves in such a way as to
   deserve and retain the confidence of Ministers and to be able
   to establish the same relationship with those whom they
   may be required to serve in some future Administration.
   They should comply with restrictions on their political
   activities. The conduct of civil servants should be such that
   Ministers and potential future Ministers can be sure that
   confidence can be freely given, and that the Civil Service
   will conscientiously fulfil its duties and obligations to, and
   impartially assist, advise and carry out the policies of, the
   duly constituted Government.

10. Civil servants should not without authority disclose official information which has been communicated in confidence within Government, or received in confidence from others. Nothing in the Code should be taken as overriding existing statutory or common law obligations to keep confidential, or to disclose, certain information. They should not seek to frustrate or influence the policies, decisions or actions of Government by the unauthorised, improper or premature disclosure outside the Government of any information to which they have had access as civil servants.

11. Where a civil servant believes he or she is being required to act in a way which:
    - is illegal, improper, or unethical;
    - is in breach of constitutional convention or a professional code;
    - may involve possible maladministration; or
    - is otherwise inconsistent with this Code;

    he or she should report the matter in accordance with procedures laid down in departmental guidance or rules of conduct. A civil servant should also report to the appropriate authorities evidence of criminal or unlawful activity by others and may also report in accordance with departmental procedures if he or she becomes aware of other breaches of this Code or is required to act in a way which, for him or her, raises a fundamental issue of conscience.

12. Where a civil servant has reported a matter covered in paragraph 11 in accordance with procedures laid down in departmental guidance or rules of conduct and believes that the response does not represent a reasonable response to the grounds of his or her concern, he or she may report the matter in writing to the Civil Service Commissioners.

13. Civil servants should not seek to frustrate the policies, decisions or actions of Government by declining to take, or abstaining from, action which flows from ministerial decisions. Where a matter cannot be resolved by the procedures set out in paragraph 11 and 12 above, on a basis which the civil servant concerned is able to accept, he or she should either carry out his or her instructions, or resign from the Civil Service. Civil servants should continue to observe their duties of confidentiality after they have left Crown employment.

References

Official publications are listed in a separate sequence below.

Albrow, Martin, 1970, *Bureaucracy*, Macmillan.

Bailey, Stephen J., 1993, 'Public Choice Theory and the Reform of Local Government in Britain: From Government to Governance', *Public Policy and Administration*, vol. 8(2), pp. 7–24.

Baines, Priscilla, 1995, 'Financial Accountability: Agencies and Audit', in Giddings, 1995, pp. 95–117.

Birch, A.H., 1964, *Representative and Responsible Government*, Allen and Unwin.

Blackstone, 1825, 16th edn, *Commentaries on the Laws of England*, J. Butterworth.

Bogdanor, Vernon, 1994, 'Ministers, Civil Servants and the Constitution', *Government and Opposition*, vol. 29, pp. 676–95.

Bosanquet, Nick, 1983, *After the New Right*, Dartmouth Publishing.

Buchanan, James and Tullock, Gordon, 1962, *The Calculus of Consent*, University of Michigan Press.

Butler, Robin, 1994, 'Reinventing British Government', *Public Administration*, vol. 72, pp. 263–70.

Campbell, Colin and Peters, B. Guy, 1988, 'The Politics/Administration Dichotomy: Death or Merely Change?', *Governance*, vol. 1, pp. 79–99.

Day, P. and Klein, R., 1987, *Accountabilities – Five Public Services*, Tavistock Publications.

de Smith, S.A. and Brazier, Rodney, 1994, 7th edn, *Constitutional and Administrative Law*, Penguin.

de Smith, S.A., Lord Woolf and Jorrell, Jeffrey, 1995, 5th edn, *Judicial Review of Administrative Action*, Sweet and Maxwell.

Dicey, A.V., 1885, 10th edn 1959, *Introduction to the Study of the Law of the Constitution*, Macmillan.

Doig, Alan, 1995, 'Mixed Signals? Public Sector Change and the Proper Conduct of Public Business', *Public Administration*, vol. 75, pp. 191–212.

Dorrell, Stephen, 1992, 'Redefining the Mixed Economy', speech to Centre for Policy Studies, 23 November 1992.

Drewry, Gavin and Butcher, Tony, 1991, 2nd edn, *The Civil Service Today*, Blackwell.

Dunleavy, Patrick, 1986, 'Topics in British Politics', in Drucker *et al.*, 1986, pp. 329–72.

Dunleavy, Patrick, 1989, 'The Architecture of the British Central State', *Public Administration*, vol. 67, two parts, Autumn and Winter issues.

Dunleavy, Patrick, and O'Leary, Brendan, 1987, *Theories of the State*, Macmillan.

Elder, Neil, 1970, *Government in Sweden*, Pergamon Press.

Evans, Paul, 1995, 'Members of Parliament and Agencies: Parliamentary Questions', in Giddings, 1995, pp. 119–37.

Finer, S.E., 1956, 'The Individual Responsibility of Ministers', *Public Administration*, vol. 34, pp. 377–96.

Freedland, M., 1996, 'The rule against delegation and the *Carltona* doctrine in an agency context', *Public Law*, pp. 19–30.

Friedman, Milton, 1962, *Capitalism and Freedom*, University of Chicago Press.

Friedman, Milton, 1975, *Unemployment or Inflation?*, Institute of Economic Affairs.

Fry, Geoffrey K., 1993, 'Developments in Civil Service Pay Since the Megaw Report', *Public Policy and Administration*, vol. 8, pp. 4–19.

Gamble, Andrew, 1994, 2nd edn, *The Free Economy and the Strong State: The Politics of Thatcherism*, Macmillan.

Ganz, Gabriele, 1987, *Quasi-Legislation: Recent Developments in Secondary Legislation*, Sweet and Maxwell.

Giddings, Philip (ed.), 1995, *Parliamentary Accountability: A Study of Parliament and Executive Agencies*, Macmillan.

Goodin, Robert, 1982, 'Rational Politicians and Rational Bureaucrats in Washington and Whitehall', *Public Administration*, vol. 60, pp. 32–41.

Greaves, H.R.G., 1947, *The Civil Service in the Changing State*, Harrap.

Greer, P., 1994, *Transforming Central Government: The Next Steps Initiative*, Open University Press.

Hansard Society Commission on the Legislative Process, 1992, *Making the Law*, Hansard Society.

Harden, Ian, 1992, *The Contracting State*, Open University Press.

Hayek, Friedrich von, 1944, *The Road to Serfdom*, Routledge.

Hayek, Friedrich von, 1960, *The Constitution of Liberty*, Routledge.

Hayek, Friedrich von, 1973–9, 3 vols, *Law, Legislation and Liberty*, Routledge.

Hewart (the Lord Hewart of Bury), 1929, *The New Despotism*, Ernest Benn.

Holdsworth, W.S., 1924, *History of English Law* (eds Goodhart, A.C. and Hanbury, H.S., 1966), Methuen, Sweet and Maxwell.

Hood, Christopher, 1991, 'A Public Management for All Seasons', *Public Administration*, vol. 69, pp. 3–20.

Jenkins, Simon, 1993, 'Sir Humphrey has a Place', *The Times*, 24 November.

Jordan, Grant, 1994, ' "Reinventing Government": But Will it Work?', *Public Administration*, vol. 72, pp. 271–9.

JUSTICE, 1971, *Administration Under Law* (Report of a Committee of JUSTICE: Chairman, Keith Goodfellow QC), Stevens.

JUSTICE–All Souls Review, 1988, *Administrative Justice: Some Necessary Reforms* (Report of the Committee of the JUSTICE–All Souls Review of Administrative Law in the United Kingdom: Chairman, Patrick Neill QC), Clarendon Press.

Kavanagh, Dennis, 1987, *Thatcherism and British Politics*, Oxford University Press.

Lester, Anthony, Mackie, Lindsay and Renshall, Michael, 1994, *What Price Hansard?* (King Hall Paper 1), Hansard Society.

Lewis, Norman, 1993, *How to Reinvent British Government*, European Policy Forum.

Lewis, Norman and Birkinshaw, Patrick, 1993, *When Citizens Complain*, Open University Press.

Lewis, Norman and Longley, Diane, 1994, 'Ethics and the Public Service' [1994] *Public Law*, pp. 596–608.

Loughlin, Martin, 1992, *Public Law and Political Theory*, Clarendon Press.

Low, Sidney, 1904, *The Governance of England*, Fisher Unwin.

Lundvik, U., 1983a, 'New Zealand', in Caiden, G. (ed.), *International Handbook of the Ombudsman*, Greenwood Press, pp. 134–44.

Lundvik, U., 1983b, 'Sweden', in Caiden, G. (ed.), *International Handbook of the Ombudsman*, Greenwood Press, pp. 179–85.

Magill, J.W., 1994, *Westminster City Council Audit of Accounts 1987/88 and Subsequent Years: Designated Sales* (Note of the Appointed Auditor's Provisional Findings and Views), Touche Ross.

Magill, J.W., 1996, *Westminster City Council Audit of Accounts 1987/88–1994/95: Designated Sales*, Deloitte Touche.

Marshall, Geoffrey, 1984, *Constitutional Conventions*, Clarendon Press.

Massey, Andrew, 1995, 'Civil Service Reform and Accountability', *Public Policy and Administration*, vol. 10, pp. 16–33.

McDonald, Oonagh, 1992a, *Swedish Models*, IPPR.

McDonald, Oonagh, 1992b, *The Future of Whitehall*, Weidenfeld and Nicolson.

McEldowney, John, 1994a, 'The control of public expenditure', in Jowell, Jeffrey and Oliver, Dawn (eds), *The Changing Constitution*, 3rd edn, Oxford University Press, pp. 175–207.

McEldowney, John, 1994b, *Public Law*, Sweet and Maxwell.

Megarry, R.E., 1944, 'Administrative Quasi-Legislation', vol. 60, *Law Quarterly Review*, p. 125, ff and 218 ff.

Metcalfe, Les, 1993, 'Conviction Politics and Dynamic Conservatism: Mrs Thatcher's Managerial Revolution', *International Political Science Review*, vol. 14, pp. 351–71.

Natzler, David and Silk, Paul, 1995, 'Departmental Select Committees and the Next Steps Programme', in Giddings, 1995, pp. 71–94.

Niskanen, William, 1971, *Bureaucracy and Representative Government*, Aldine-Atherton.

Niskanen, William, 1973, *Bureaucracy: Servant or Master?*, Institute of Economic Affairs.

OECD, 1990, *Survey of Public Management Developments*, 1990, OECD.

OECD, 1993, *Survey of Public Management Developments*, 1993, OECD.

OECD, 1994, *Public Management Developments: Update 1994*, OECD.

Oliver, Dawn, 1993, 'The Case of the Shorthandwriters', [1993] *Public Law*, pp. 214–20.

Oliver, Dawn and Austin, Rodney, 1987, 'Political and Constitutional Implications of the Westland Affair', *Parliamentary Affairs*, vol. 40, pp. 20–41.

Olson, Mancur, 1965, *The Logic of Collective Action*, Harvard University Press.

Olson, Mancur, 1982, *The Rise and Decline of Nations*, Yale University Press.

Osborne, David and Gaebler, Ted, 1992, *Reinventing Government: How the Entrepreneurial Spirit is Transforming the Public Sector*, Addison-Wesley.

Palmer, Geoffrey, 1987, *Unbridled Power*, Oxford University Press.

Pannick, David, 1992, 'Who is Subject to Judicial Review and in Respect of What?', [1992] *Public Law*, pp. 1–7.

Pliatzky, Leo, 1992, 'Quangos and Agencies', *Public Administration*, vol. 70, pp. 555–63.

Power, Michael, 1994, *The Audit Explosion*, Demos.

Rhodes, R.A.W., 1991, 'Introduction', *Public Administration*, vol. 69 (special issue on the New Public Management).

Rhodes, R.A.W., 1994a, 'The Hollowing Out of the State: The Changing Nature of the Public Service in Britain', *Political Quarterly*, vol. 65, pp. 138–51.

Rhodes, R.A.W., 1994b, 'Reinventing Excellence: Or How Best-Sellers Thwart the Search for Lessons to Transform the Public Sector', *Public Administration*, vol. 72, pp. 281–9.

Richardson, J., 1982, 'Programme Evaluation in Britain and Sweden', *Parliamentary Affairs*, vol. 35, pp. 160–80.

Ridley, F.F., 1984, 'The Citizen Against Authority: British Approaches to the Redress of Grievances,' *Parliamentary Affairs*, vol. 37, pp. 1–32.

Roberts, Simon and Pollitt, Christopher, 1994, 'Audit or Evaluation? A National Audit Office VFM Study', *Public Administration*, vol. 72, pp. 527–49.

Sisson, C.H., 1959, *The Spirit of British Administration*, Faber and Faber.

Stewart, John and Walsh, Kieron, 1992, 'Change in the Management of Public Services', *Public Administration*, vol. 70, pp. 499–518.

Thatcher, Margaret, 1993, *The Downing Street Years*, HarperCollins.

Tullock, Gordon, 1965, *The Politics of Bureaucracy*, Public Affairs Press.

Wade, H.W.R. and Forsyth, C.F., 1994, 7th edn, *Administrative Law*, Clarendon Press.

Waldegrave, William, 1993, *Public Service and the Future: Reforming Britain's Bureaucracies*, Conservative Political Centre.

Weir, Stuart and Hall, Wendy (eds), 1994, *Ego Trip: Extra-Governmental Organisations in the United Kingdom and their Accountability* (Democratic Audit Paper No. 2), Human Rights Centre, University of Essex.

White, Fidelma, Harden, Ian and Donnelly, Katy, 1994, *The Changing Constitutional Role of Public Sector Audit*, University of Sheffield.

Wistrich, E., 1992, 'Restructuring Government New Zealand Style', *Public Administration*, vol. 70, pp. 119–35.

Woodhouse, Diana, 1994, *Ministers and Parliament*, Oxford University Press.

OFFICIAL PUBLICATIONS IN APPROXIMATE CHRONOLOGICAL ORDER

Northcote Trevelyan Report, 1854, reprinted as an Appendix to the Fulton Report, 1968, below.

Fulton Report, 1968, *The Civil Service*, Cmnd 3638, HMSO.

Expenditure Committee, 1976–77. Eleventh Report. *The Civil Service*, HC 535.

The Financial Management Initiative, 1982, Cmnd 8616, HMSO.

TCSC, 1985–6, Seventh Report from the Treasury and Civil Service Committee. *Civil Servants and Ministers: Duties and Responsibilities*, HC 92.

Defence Committee, 1985–6, Fourth Report from the Defence Committee, *Westland plc: The Government's Decision-Making*, HC 519.

TCSC, 1987–8, New Zealand Treasury, 1987, *Government Management Brief to the Incoming Government*. Eighth Report of the Treasury and Civil Service Committee, *Civil Service Management Reform: The Next Steps*, HC 494.

Improving Management in Government: The Next Steps, 1988, Cabinet Office.

TCSC, 1989–90, Eighth Report of the Treasury and Civil Service Committee, *Progress in the Next Steps Initiative*, HC 481.

The Financing and Accountability of Next Steps Agencies, 1989, Cm 914, HMSO.

Improving Management in Government – The Next Steps Agencies: Review 1990, 1990, Cm 1261, HMSO.

Select Committee on Procedure, 1990–1, Third Report from the Select Committee on Procedure, *Parliamentary Questions*, HC 178.

TCSC, 1990–1, Seventh Report from the Treasury and Civil Service Committee, *The Next Steps Initiative*, HC 496.

National Audit Office, 1991, *Creating and Safeguarding Jobs in Wales*.

The Citizen's Charter: Raising the Standard, 1991, Cm 1599, HMSO.

Competing for Quality: Buying Better Public Services, 1991, Cm 1730, HMSO.

Improving Management in Government – The Next Steps Agencies: Review 1991, 1991, Cm 1760, HMSO.

PCA Committee, 1991–2, Second Report from the Select Committee on the Parliamentary Commissioner for Administration, *The Implication of the Citizen's Charter for the Work of the Parliamentary Commissioner for Administration*, HC 158.

Improving Management in Government – The Next Steps Agencies: Review 1992, 1992, Cm 2110, HMSO.

The Citizen's Charter First Report, 1992; Cm 2101.

Treasury, 1992, *Executive Agencies – A Guide to Setting Targets and Measuring Performance*, HMSO.

National Audit Office, 1992, The Vehicle Inspectorate.

Questions of Procedure for Ministers, 1992, revised 1994 and 1996, Cabinet Office.

PAC, 1992–3, Nineteenth Report from the Public Accounts Committee, *The Vehicle Inspectorate: Progress as the First Executive Agency*, HC 118.

TCSC, 1993, Sixth Report from the Treasury and Civil Service Committee, *The Role of the Civil Service: Interim Report*, HC 390. vol. I, Report; vol. II, Minutes of Evidence and Appendices.

Employment Select Committee, 1993, *Minutes of Evidence Taken Before the Select Committee for Employment on the Work of the Employment Service*, 31 March, HC 598-i.

Parliamentary Commissioner for Administration, 1992–3, Sixth Report – Session 1992–93, *Delays in Handling Disability Living Allowance Claims*, HC 652.

Treasury Minute on the 19th, 20th, 23rd and 25th Reports of the Public Accounts Committee session 1992/93 [concerning various executive agencies], 1993, Cm 2175.

Next Steps Review 1993, 1993, Cm 2430, HMSO.

Employment Department, 1993, *Employment Service Memorandum of Financial Arrangements*.

The Government's Guide to Market Testing, 1993, Efficiency Unit, OPSS.

Employment Services, 1993, *A Framework Document for the Agency*.

Employment Services, 1993, *Benefits for Unemployed People*.

Open Government, 1993, Cm 2290, HMSO.

Audit Commission, n.d., *Citizen's Charter Indicators: Charting a Course*, 1994, Audit Commission.

The Government's Guide to Market Testing, 1993, HMSO.

TCSC, 1993–4, Fifth Report from the Treasury and Civil Service Committee, *The Role of The Civil Service*, HC 27. vol. I, Report; vol. II, Minutes of Evidence; vol. III, Appendices to the Minutes of Evidence.

Parliamentary Commissioner for Administration, 1993–4, *Annual Report for 1993*, HC 290.

PCA Committee, 1994–5, Third Report – Session 1994–95, *Investigation of Complaints against the Child Support Agency*, HC 135.

Next Steps Review 1994, 1994, Cm 2750, HMSO.

Armstrong Memorandum: The Duties and Responsibilities of Civil Servants in Relation to Ministers, 1987/1993–4, Note by the Head of the Civil Service, Sir Robert Armstrong, HC Deb., 2 December 1987 and (revised) HC 27–II, 1993–4.

PAC, 1993–4, Eighth Report from the Committee of Public Accounts, *The Proper Conduct of Public Business*, HC 154.

PAC, 1993–4, Seventeenth Report of the Public Accounts Committee, *Pergau Hydro-electric Project*, HC 155.

The Civil Service: Continuity and Change, 1994, Cm 2627, HMSO.

Foreign Affairs Committee, 1993–4, Third Report of the Foreign Affairs Committee, *Public Expenditure: Pergau Hydro-electric Project, Malaysia, the Aid and Trade Provisions and Related Matters*, HC 271.

PCA Committee, 1994–5, *Fourth Report of the Select Committee on the Parliamentary Commissioner for Administration*, HC 394.

The Citizen's Charter: Second Report: 1994, 1994, Cm 2540.

Treasury Minute, 1993, Cm 2175, HMSO.

Departmental Evidence and Response to Select Committees (known as the Osmotherly Rules), 1994, Cabinet Office.

PCA Committee, 1994–5, Third Report from the Select Committee on the Parliamentary Commissioner for Administration, *The Child Support Agency*, HC 199.

Next Steps Review 1994, 1994, Cm 2750, HMSO.

Parliamentary Commissioner for Administration, 1994–5, Second Report – Session 1994–95, *Access to Official Information: The First Eight Months*, HC 91.

PCA Committee, 1994–5, *Fourth Report of the Select Committee of the Parliamentary Commissioner for Administration*, HC 394.

The Civil Service: Taking Forward Continuity and Change, 1995, Cm 2748, HMSO.

The Nolan Report, 1995, *First Report of the Committee on Standards in Public Life*, Cm 2850, HMSO.

The Government's Response to the First Report from the Committee on Standards in Public Life, 1995, Cm 2931, HMSO.

The Learmont Report, *Review of Prison Service Security in England and Wales and The Escape from Parkhurst Prison on Tuesday 3rd January 1995*, 1995, Cm. 3020, HMSO.

The Civil Service Code, 1995, HL Deb., 30 October 1995, cols 146–8.

Next Steps Review 1995, 1996, Cm 3164, HMSO.

Sir Richard Scott, 1996, *Report of the Inquiry into the Export of Defence Equipment and Dual-Use Goods to Iraq and Related Prosecutions*, HC 115.

Parliamentary Commissioner for Administration, 1995–6, Fourth Report – Session 1995–96 and *Annual Report for 1995*, HC 296.

HMSO Trading Fund Accounts 1995, HC 349.

Index